The Bride's Year Ahead

❧ I want to thank all the brides and grooms for allowing me to be a part of their special day. The experience has allowed me the opportunity to share these wonderful photographs with our audience of future brides.

I also want to thank Monica Dietrich, my agent and friend; without her, we would just have pictures.

CAROL ROSS

Published by Ronnie Sellers Productions, Inc.

Copyright 2003 © PM Design Group, Inc.
Photography 2003 © Carol Ross
Text by Marguerite Smolen
All rights reserved.

Project Editor: Robin Haywood
Editor: Elani Torres
Cover Design: Patti Urban
Interior Design: Nina Barnett

P.O. Box 818, Portland, Maine 04104
For ordering information:
Toll free: 800-MAKEFUN (800-625-3386)
Fax: (207) 772-6814
Visit our Web site: www.makefun.com
E-mail: rsp@rsvp.com

ISBN: 1-56906-547-0
Library of Congress Control Number: 2003096759

Printed in China

The Bride's Year Ahead

THE ULTIMATE MONTH-BY-MONTH
WEDDING PLANNER

Photography by Carol Ross
Text by Marguerite Smolen

RONNIE SELLERS PRODUCTIONS
PORTLAND, MAINE

contents

introduction

*T*he moment you've dreamed of has finally come. You've found that special someone who loves you just as you are, who will stick with you through good times and bad, now and forever: You're getting married. Of course you want to share your newfound happiness with family and friends, to honor your commitment to join together by planning the celebration of a lifetime. If you're like most engaged couples, though, the prospect of orchestrating such a big event is overwhelming. Wouldn't it be wonderful to have a wedding planner available 24 hours a day to help you prepare for this most important occasion?

Well, now you do. This compact volume, designed with busy couples in mind, contains all the essential information you need to plan a wedding. Starting with the ceremony, moving on to the reception, and through to the honeymoon, it provides step-by-step instructions on how to create an event that is every bit as unique as the love you share. In the following pages, you'll learn when you should book a reception hall, what questions to ask a caterer, and how to get the most music for your money. You'll find out how to buy a wedding gown that suits your style and flatters your figure. We'll help you to personalize your wedding with creative ideas. And we'll share many of the secrets bridal professionals prefer to keep to themselves.

To make planning your special day both easy and fun, we've broken the whole, complicated process up into simple steps and organized these steps into a timeline. Each tabbed section of this book covers one month in the wedding planning process and opens with a to-do list for that month. Also included are checklists, worksheets, questions-and-answers, and other useful information designed to keep you on track with a minimum of effort. You can keep frequently dialed numbers handy in the Notes section at the back of the book. Use the Monthly Planner calendar on each tab page to keep track of appointments and booking dates.

To make the most of the information contained in this book, skim it first, cover-to-cover. Once you have an overview of the entire planning process, you can get started planning your own wedding by utilizing the information in the first chapter. The book is divided into twelve chapters, because most couples plan their weddings a year in advance. If you have less than a year to plan your celebration, you can combine the activities in multiple months and still have a workable plan — although a somewhat abbreviated one!

Your wedding day should be a fun occasion, providing you with memories to cherish for years to come. *The Bride's Year Ahead* is designed not only to help you to achieve this happy ending, but also to make the months of planning beforehand an enjoyable adventure, too.

Chapter 1: TWELVE MONTHS AHEAD

Planning for Success

Monthly Planner

Sunday	Monday	Tuesday	Wednesday	Thursday	Friday	Saturday

Chapter 1: TWELVE MONTHS AHEAD

Planning for Success

You want your wedding to be perfect, complete with a moving ceremony, beautiful gown, and a reception that captures the essence of the love you and your intended share. Careful planning at the start of your engagement will help turn your hopes into reality.

THIS MONTH'S TO-DO LIST

1. Meet with the officiant.

2. Set the wedding date.

3. Prepare a budget.

4. Book a reception hall or hire a caterer.

As a newly engaged couple, perhaps you feel as if you are riding on an emotional roller coaster: There is the thrill of being betrothed and the joy of thinking of a future with your partner. At the same time, you may experience stomach-churning anxiety over wanting everything to come off perfectly . . . even though you've never planned such a big and important event before. And then there is the advice you receive — some appreciated, perhaps some unasked for — from everyone who hears about your intention to marry. Don't worry. Planning a wedding can be a smooth operation. But it is important that you take time to think about what you want and to plan the desired outcome with care.

If both of you are very religious, a meeting with a member of your clergy comes first. As officiant at a sacred event, the priest (or minister or rabbi) most likely will have certain constraints regarding the ceremony time and place. These constraints in turn may affect where and when the wedding and reception can be held. In addition, your religion may require that couples complete classes to prepare for marriage. For some religions, it is not unusual for these marriage "prep" classes to take six months or even a year to complete.

If you are not religious, but consider yourself to be spiritual, you will also want to give some thought to the sacred aspects of a wedding. Do you and your spouse-to-be come from different faiths? Do you need to reconcile any differences? Will you both be married in the same faith or by different sets of clergy? If you both are okay with being married by a nondenominational minister (there are many who specialize in weddings) or a justice of the peace, then booking an officiant in advance may not be necessary. You still may want to consider attending some counseling or a marriage-prep course, however, to help make the adjustment to marriage easier in the months after you wed.

Once you have cleared the date with the participating clergy (or decided on an option that does not involve an organized religion), your next priority should be to come up with general guidelines for the type of wedding you want to have and the budget you will be working with. Deciding on the type of wedding is important because it will help to

QUESTIONS TO ASK A CHURCH OFFICIANT

🌼 What is your policy regarding booking a wedding?

🌼 How far in advance should we contact you?

🌼 Are there any required meetings or coursework?

🌼 What is church policy regarding interfaith marriages? Will you officiate together with clergy from another faith?

🌼 What dates and times is the church available?

🌼 Will you officiate in a place other than the church?

🌼 What restrictions does the church have? How many people can it hold? Are we allowed to take pictures or to videotape the ceremony? If not, can we take pictures before and after the ceremony?

🌼 Are decorations allowed?

🌼 Is there any restriction on the type of clothing that must be worn? (Some religions may not approve of the current fashion for strapless bridal gowns.)

🌼 Is there a set ceremony, rite, or ritual that must be followed?

🌼 Can we write our own ceremony or personalize the ceremony in any way?

🌼 Does the church allow outside musicians? Are any restrictions placed on the type of music or number of musicians? Does the church have any musicians or vocalists that are available for the ceremony?

🌼 Can guests throw birdseed or rice as the couple exits the church?

🌼 Is there a room where the bride can dress?

🌼 What is the cost to book the church and any of its musicians?

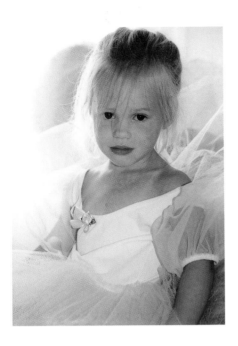

eliminate inappropriate venues and resources, thus leaving you more time to investigate possibilities that are realistic for you. Figuring out the total dollar amount you can spend for your big day will save you time for the same reason. Venues and service providers that exceed your budget can be eliminated quickly, leaving more time for careful shopping among those who are within your means.

Don't worry about making a detailed spending plan for every item just yet. For now, just determine a total dollar cost. You will not be able to identify an allowance for an item until you have shopped around a bit. As you start to compare prices during this first month, you will begin to refine your priorities. By month's end, you should have a very firm idea of how much you will spend on each aspect of the wedding. Until then, we suggest using a pencil to fill out the budget worksheet at the end of this chapter!

No matter what figure you come up

WHAT'S YOUR WEDDING STYLE?

Of course, you can mix and mingle wedding styles. But for those couples who don't know what kind of wedding they want, here are some ideas for finding a style.

Country: Held outdoors in a rural environment or in a summerhouse; underneath a rose-covered arch or gazebo; or indoors in a barn, cabin, or rustic country house; buckets filled with wildflowers; a horse-drawn cart; barbecue or picnic fare. The bride will wear a mid-calf or ankle-length dress without a train and a big picture hat or floral wreath. The maids will wear print cotton frocks. The groom will wear a suit or jacket and tie with brown or gray trousers.

Historic / Theme: Popular ideas include Victorian, Civil War, Wild West, Maritime, Medieval, and Broadway musicals such as *The Phantom of the Opera* — but your imagination can only add to the list! Once you've decided on a theme, you can recreate it in as much or as little detail as you wish — down to dressing in costume and serving food based on historic menus. Many outfits cater to costuming wedding parties. (See Resources.)

Urban Sophisticate: Elegant big-city hotel wedding characterized by formal linens; an open bar with a four- or five-course meal; floral "trees" or "towers" on the tables, allowing people to see each other through the super-tall glass or acrylic vases or pedestals; and big band or orchestral dance music. The bride's gown will end in a long train (or she'll remove it and convert her dress to a strapless formal), while her groom (and any male guests) will wear white or black tie. The bridesmaids will wear black cocktail dresses.

(continued on next page)

Avant-garde: Held in a museum, warehouse, or other artistic venue, this wedding will feature theatrical set decorations, strolling performers for entertainment, and a buffet or variety of food stations providing diverse fare. Everyone dresses creatively!

Clubby: Celebrate your wedding in exclusive surrounds on a small scale at a club in town. You either belong to one or can access a private club that rents to outsiders — a women's, art, or some other social club. The atmosphere is more like someone's home than a standard banquet hall. You can personalize it — but still keep a traditional flavor. The groom wears a traditional morning coat or a navy blue blazer with gray pants, white shirt, and tie, and the bride wears a semiformal dress. If the groom is in the military, he may wear his dress uniform.

Ethnic: Celebrate diversity in a museum or other location that captures your heritage, be it African-American, Asian, or Celtic. Your food, attire, and decor will be informed by the traditions of your culture. Guests will treasure this opportunity to feast their senses on the flavors and atmosphere of a remote place or time. If you incorporate several traditions into your celebration, you can make it a true multicultural event!

Traditional: At a catering hall or country club. Mom and Dad's generation will happily dig into the prime rib, and you'll be able to get linens in your "wedding color." The pace is pleasingly predictable, the atmosphere is chaste and romantic, and the clockwork efficiency of an experienced staff (perhaps one that has watched you grow up) ensures that everyone attending will have a good time. The bride will wear a traditional white wedding gown with a chapel train, the groom will wear a tuxedo, and the bridesmaids will wear dresses to match the table linens.

with, if you're like most brides, the majority of your budget will be spent on the reception. So, this month, you will make visiting reception halls and caterers a priority. Another reason for making the reception this month's priority is that, generally speaking, you will have to work quickly to book a reception hall or caterer, especially if you are thinking of a venue that is very popular. Most banquet halls and hotels are booked a year in advance, especially during the most popular months for weddings (in most parts of the country, these are June and September). Of course, if you are working two or more years in advance, then you can likely take your pick of all but the most famous, big-city hotels. Use the worksheets in this chapter to make a careful comparison of each of the venues before deciding which one you will book.

save money on your reception by . . .

Limiting the guest list to 40 people or fewer. A smaller reception will allow you to choose from among many more places, and makes possible intimate (less expensive) venues, such as local restaurants and bed-and-breakfasts.

Getting married on a weekday. Keep in mind that work obligations may prevent some guests from sharing in your celebration. If this is unacceptable to you, then a weekend wedding makes better sense.

Choosing a less popular time and day, if you decide to hold the wedding on a weekend. Saturday nights tend to be most popular, followed by Saturday afternoons. A wedding breakfast or brunch is not as popular as an evening dinner and reception, but can still be quite lovely. Sunday is typically less popular than Saturdays, if only because most people need to get back to work on Monday.

Getting married during a time of year that is not especially in demand. For example, most reception halls are looking for business in late January and early February (which is one reason so many bridal shows are held in those months).

Booking a facility that has not yet opened or has been opened for only a short time. New businesses may have openings to fill and a reputation to establish.

Questions to Ask a Reception Hall and Caterer:

	VENDOR NAME:
What is the maximum number of guests a room can hold for a sit-down meal? For a buffet? For cocktails and hors d'oeuvres?	
How many wedding receptions do you cater in the same time period? Will our wedding party have exclusive use of your facility?	
Is alcohol allowed? If so, is it BYOB or must it be purchased through the facility? Does the facility offer a five- or four-hour open bar?	
Is a champagne (or sparkling wine) toast included in the price?	
Is a wedding cake included in the price? Can I order my cake elsewhere?	
How many hors d'oeuvres do you make for each guest? How many different varieties of hors d'oeuvres are included in the price?	
Can I have a Viennese dessert table if I am willing to pay extra?	
What type of coffee service is provided?	
Are personnel charges included (for waitstaff, bartenders, maître d', master of ceremonies, wedding planner)?	
Is there a coat check?	
What type of service do you supply (for example: French-plated tableside; American-plated in the kitchen and brought to the table; ultra-class French-prepared and plated within view)?	
Is valet parking available?	
Do you offer a bridal hospitality room, in which the wedding party may freshen up, or overnight bridal couple accommodations?	
Are flowers included? Is there a house florist, or may I bring my own floral arrangements?	
When is the deposit due?	
When is the balance due?	
Are taxes and gratuities included in the fee?	
What are your overtime charges and how can they be avoided?	
Is liability insurance available?	
What is your cancellation policy? Is cancellation insurance available?	

VENDOR NAME:	VENDOR NAME:

Don't forget — get all costs in writing and read any contract carefully before signing it.
Better yet, have an unemotional, detached (but trustworthy) third-party read the contracts for you!

ITEM	COST	NOTES
REHEARSAL DINNER		
Rehearsal Dinner: Site		
Rehearsal Dinner: Food and Service		
Rehearsal Dinner: Liquor		
Rehearsal Dinner: Entertainment		
Rehearsal Dinner: Other		
Transportation to Rehearsal Dinner		
Attendants' Gifts		
CEREMONY		
Ceremony: Site		
Officiant		
Decorations		
Flowers		
Music		
Service Assistance		
Programs		
Pew Cards		
Certificate		
Registration Fee		
Birdseed/Favors		
Transportation to Ceremony		
COCKTAIL PARTY		
Cocktail Party: Food and Service		
Cocktail Party: Liquor		
Cocktail Party: Entertainment		
Cocktail Party: Decor		
Cocktail Party: Flowers		
Transportation to Cocktail Party		

ITEM	COST	NOTES
RECEPTION		
Reception: Hall Site		
Reception: Food and Service		
Reception: Liquor		
Reception: Decor		
Reception: Flowers		
Favors		
Wedding Cake		
Viennese Pastry Table		
Valet Parking		
Transportation to Reception		
Photography		
Reception Entertainment		
Wedding Planner		
Master of Ceremonies		
Florist: Bridal Flowers		
Florist: Wedding Party Flowers		
Florist: Groom and Groomsmen		
Florist: Parents of Bride and Groom		
Bridal Gown		
Tuxedo		
Bridesmaids' Dresses		
Groomsmen Attire		
Honeymoon		
Gifts		
Other:		
Other:		
Other:		
Other:		
Other:		

RECEPTION HALL COMPARISON WORKSHEET

RECEPTION HALL NAME AND ADDRESS	CONTACT NAME AND PHONE NUMBER	GUEST CAPACITY	PRICE RANGE PER GUEST (minimum/ maximum)	TYPE OF PACKAGE (e.g., 5-course sit-down, food stations, buffet)

SEPARATE ROOM FOR COCKTAILS?	RATIO OF SERVERS TO GUESTS	DATES AND TIMES AVAILABLE	CEREMONY FACILITY	NOTES:

Chapter 2: ELEVEN MONTHS AHEAD

Beginning with Essentials

This month, plan to announce the engagement to distant family and friends. Because you booked the site last month, you'll have a ready answer when they ask you when and where the big event will take place!

THIS MONTH'S TO-DO LIST

1. Announce your engagement.

2. Choose the wedding party.

3. Book a photographer and videographer.

4. Hire musicians.

Reserving the site and announcing the engagement are the first steps in producing the wedding of your dreams. You'll want music to set the mood and a fabulous photographer to capture those memorable moments. The best photographers and musicians get booked almost as early as the reception halls. Now is the time to line up the photo professional who will create an album as beautiful as your memories of this event and a band or DJ that will make the perfect soundtrack to your nuptials.

Announcing the engagement formally is a time-honored wedding tradition. But prior to announcing the event in public, it is advisable to let close family (parents, especially) and friends know the good news. It is very easy to hurt a parent's, best friend's, or loved one's feelings by letting him or her find out from someone other than yourself that you are planning to get married.

Once you have personally informed those in your intimate circle that you are engaged, it can be announced in public. Traditionally, parents throw the couple's engagement party; today, however, it is not unusual for a close friend, or even the couple themselves, to throw a celebratory affair.

sample engagement announcement . . .

Bride's Full Name to Wed Groom's Full Name

[Bride's Parents] of [Town] announce the engagement of their daughter, [Bride's First Name] to [Groom's Full Name] of [Town, State.] The couple will be married on [Wedding Date].

Miss [Bride's Last Name] graduated from [Name of High School] and [List Additional Degrees and School/ University Affiliations]. She is a [Occupation].

[If the bride is a member of a prominent family, family information goes here.]

Mr. [Groom's Full Name], son of [List Title and Names of Groom's Parents], was graduated from [Name of High School] and [List Additional Degrees and School/University Affiliations]. He is a [Occupation].

[If the groom is a member of a prominent family, family information goes here.]

- Engagement parties are held prior to publishing an engagement announcement in the newspaper.

- The engagement announcement should be printed in the newspaper the day after the engagement party.

- Call the newspaper to obtain information about how to announce your engagement no later than two months in advance. Most newspapers have a recorded message that will tell you what you need to know to announce your wedding; others may have a form for you to fill out and mail in.

- Read the announcements of engagements in your local paper and copy the format and wording closely. Unless you are a celebrity, or have an unusual story to tell, existing write-ups will give you a realistic picture of what the paper is apt to publish.

- Mail your release to the appropriate person at the paper (typically the society or "women's page," sometimes called "Lifestyles" editor).

- Type your engagement announcement neatly. Include the following:
  - Correct spellings of names
  - Contact name, telephone number, and e-mail address for more information on the top of the announcement
  - The words
    FOR RELEASE ON _____ (DATE) in capital letters at the top of the page

- A professionally taken studio photograph of the bride. A head shot is preferred. An 8 x 10 portrait is preferable, but, if the photo is professionally taken, a smaller size will do.

- Attach a caption with the correct spelling of the bride's name, the date of the wedding, and the groom's name to the photo.

- Mail the announcement to the newspaper four weeks in advance in an envelope with the following words typed on the outside:
  WEDDING ANNOUNCEMENT ENCLOSED
  or PRESS MATERIALS ENCLOSED

- Follow up your "press release" mailing in two weeks with a phone call informing the editor that you sent your wedding announcement to the newspaper.

- If one parent is deceased, the living parent and his or her spouse (if s/he has remarried) announces the engagement, and a sentence acknowledging the deceased parent is inserted: "The bride is the daughter of the late [Deceased Parent's Name]."

- If the parents are divorced, the mother announces the engagement, and the father is referenced in the announcement on a separate line: "Miss [Bride's Name] also is the daughter of [Father's Title and Name]."

- In the event that parents are not alive, a close friend or relative may announce the engagement.

Choosing Your Wedding Party

Close on the heels of your engagement announcement, you'll be expected to announce the members of your bridal party. It's actually a good idea to give some thought to who you would like to be involved before you announce your engagement, since this question almost invariably arises once your plans and wedding date have been mentioned.

TITLE	DESCRIPTION	DUTIES	OUR CHOICES
Maid/Matron of Honor	Sister or close friend; may have both	Precedes bride in processional Escorted by the best man Helps arrange veil and train Holds bride's flowers during ceremony Assists bride with wedding plans and preparation Helps the bride get dressed Witnesses the signing of the wedding certificate	
Bridesmaid	Bride's close friend, sister of groom, younger female family member or relative; may have more than one	Precedes bride in processional Escorted by usher/groomsman Assists bride with wedding plans and preparation	
Best Man	Groom's brother or best friend	Helps groom with wedding preparations Organizes bachelor party Helps the groom get dressed Holds the wedding ring Witnesses the signing of the wedding certificate Holds the clergyman's fee and church fee envelopes Toasts the bride and groom	
Usher/Groomsman	Groom's close friend, brothers, relatives	Seats people at the wedding Escorts bridesmaids	
Flower Girl	Young female child	Precedes other wedding party members down the aisle, sometimes tossing petals	
Ring Bearer	Young male child	Carries the wedding rings to the altar on a pillow designed to hold them, typically with ribbons	

Few aspects of a wedding incite more emotion than wedding photos. They are a permanent record of one of life's most important milestones.

With technological developments, the wedding photography industry is rapidly evolving. Digital photography and printing and video stills are making traditional wedding albums full of beautifully printed photos a thing of the past. Today, it's common for many of the candid photos at a wedding to be taken by guests who use disposable cameras supplied by the couple. Professional photographers can more easily provide computer enhancements to photos, and often print on archival-quality (ask to be sure) paper off a printer instead of processing prints in a darkroom (ask your photographer about his or her process) or at a well-known professional lab. Videographers have access to professional editing equipment that makes it easy for them to add special effects and animations. Multimedia CDs are replacing or accompanying the traditional wedding album.

The following checklists outline important questions to ask your photographer/videographer, as well as information your photographer or videographer needs from you.

a word about ownership . . .

Read your wedding photography contract carefully. Many couples are surprised to find out that their film and the rights to reprint the photos remains with the photographer in many cases. You may find a photo of yourself in a stock image catalog or on an ad without your permission or any kind of compensation. Typically, the photographer will ask you to sign a photo release (or a clause in the contract will include language similar to that of a photo release), granting all rights to your image and likeness to the photographer. If you wish to buy "all rights" to your wedding-day photographs, expect to pay a higher fee.

Wedding Photography Checklist

Most photographers offer a variety of wedding photography packages. It is important to provide the photographer with a list of the events and people you want photographed. Use this list of standard wedding photo opportunities to compile your own.

FORMAL PORTRAITS

- Full-length bridal portrait in studio
- Close-up bridal portrait
- Full-length couple portrait in studio
- Close-up couple portrait
- Wedding party portrait in (location)
- Bride's family portrait in (location)
- Groom's family portrait in (location)
- Bride, groom, and both sets of parents
- Bride with her attendants
- Groom with his attendants
- Bride and groom with flower girl and ringbearer
- Groom's attendants
- Bride's attendants
- Bride and maid/matron of honor
- Groom and best man

LOCATION PHOTOGRAPHY

- Candid shots of wedding rehearsal
- Rehearsal dinner

ON THE DAY OF THE WEDDING:

- The bride dressing
- The groom dressing
- The bride with her parents before leaving for the ceremony
- Other:

  _____

  _____

AT THE CEREMONY SITE:

- The ceremony site exterior
- The ceremony site interior
- The bride's arrival at the ceremony
- The groom's arrival at the ceremony
- The arrival at the ceremony of the following people (list):

_____

_____

_____

_____

_____

_____

- The altar/chuppah/other
- The processional
- The following parts of the ceremony (list):

_____

_____

_____

- The recessional
- The departure of the bride and groom from the ceremony site.
- Decor (list)
- Other (list):

_____

_____

_____

PRE-RECEPTION PHOTO SHOOT LOCATION

After the ceremony and prior to the reception, many couples often elect to have their photos taken at a nearby garden, park, or other location that makes a striking photo backdrop.

_____

_____

_____

_____

RECEPTION

- Wedding party arrival at reception
- Couple's first dance
- Reception hall set-up
- Bride's dance with father
- Groom's dance with mother
- Bride's parents' dance
- Groom's parents' dance
- Cutting of the cake
- The garter
- Throwing the bouquet
- The best man's toast
- Each table (guests)
- Candid shots of the party
- Other (list):

_____

_____

_____

_____

Tips for Choosing a Photographer

Check the photographer's reputation with the Better Business Bureau (BBB).

Ask for professional credentials, such as membership in an organization. If the photographer belongs to any professional organizations, find out what code of ethics those organizations endorse. For example, Wedding Photographers International (WPI) and the Professional Photographer's Association (PPA) accredit photographers and membership in professional organizations such as these can provide some recourse if a dispute arises.

Many photographers charge a flat fee that covers your arrival at the church through the cutting of the cake. This fee can range significantly. If you don't have a lot of money to spend, get several bids and look for a photographer that provides average cost.

Get a written contract and a payment plan in three installments: one to reserve the date; a second prior to the day; and a third upon acceptance.

Supply the photographer with a list of the people and events you want the photographer to take pictures of.

Specify the name of the photographer on the contract; otherwise someone whose work you've never seen (and who may have little or no experience) may show up.

Wedding Photography Estimates

	ESTIMATE #1	ESTIMATE #2
Photographer Name/Address		
Phone Number		
Web site		
Dates and Times Available		
Standard Package Description *(number of prints and album style)*		
Standard Package Price		
Proofs Delivery Date		
Album Delivery Date		
Portrait Delivery Date		
Special Techniques		
Digital File Availability		
Traditional Printing and Processing		
Digital Printing and Processing		

ESTIMATE #3	ESTIMATE #4

Take some time to consider how music can create atmosphere and highlight the most meaningful aspects of your special day. Although most couples equate wedding music to a band or DJ for the reception, there are many other opportunities to incorporate music into your wedding. By doing so, you announce to guests that your event is truly special and something much more than an ordinary party.

Well-orchestrated wedding music is akin to the soundtrack of a good movie, framing your special occasion, signaling its beginning, middle, and end, and drawing attention to its most significant moments. A traditional scenario is to book classical or liturgical music for the ceremony, a solo pianist, harpist, or folk group or ethnic performer for a cocktail hour, and a dance band for the dinner itself.

Religious custom dictates what music is allowed in churches, so, if you are getting married in a place of worship, check with your officiant to see if there are any restrictions on what can and cannot be played during your ceremony. For example, even though many people of Irish heritage are Catholic, Catholic churches often won't allow "pagan" Celtic music, even when this is not an officially published policy. Some synagogues will allow only certain Klezmer musicians to perform, based on how authentic their repertoire is. Often, churches and synagogues will require you to use house organists, vocalists, or choirs.

Of course, if your choice of venue and officiant does not tie you to tradition, you can be as creative as you like. Couples have walked down the aisle to just about every kind of music, from Broadway show tunes to Elvis Presley, to reggae to fusion.

During the traditional American wedding, incidental music is played as guests arrive. The walk down the aisle is almost always accompanied by ceremonial music paced to dramatize the importance of the wedding procession. A fanfare of music trumpeted by a brass quintet, a triumphant march performed by the church organist, or ethnic music, such as a bagpiper or harpist for those who wish to celebrate their Celtic roots, are among the most popular choices for the wedding procession. The highlight of the ceremony itself is often accented with a solemn but joyous song rendered by a vocalist or a choir. Exit music is typically a fast-paced, celebratory instrumental or a joyous pealing of bells.

If ethnic music is not played during the ceremony, it often plays a role at the cocktail hour before the reception. This is also the time when jazz, classical, chamber music, or some other type of music difficult to dance to but favored by the couple is played. Whatever type of cocktail music you choose, however, do keep in mind that volume is important. If the music is too loud, it will disturb the process of meeting, greeting, and getting acquainted, which the cocktail hour was designed to accomplish. Cocktail music should be loud enough to set a mood and soft enough so that people can talk while it is playing.

The wedding band or DJ is the focal point of the reception music. While ceremony and cocktail music is often booked for

TIPS FOR CHOOSING A MUSICAL GROUP

Ask if the musician is planning a showcase where you can listen to the group perform.

Ask for a free demo cassette or CD.

Make sure that the musicians you hear are the ones that will be performing. Ask about the possibility of last-minute substitutions.

Verify the length of time the band will play and the frequency and number of breaks for the contract price.

Have the contract specify whether the band will be able to play longer if you change your mind at the last minute, or whether they will have to leave for another reception. If they can play longer, expect to pay an additional hourly rate. Make sure that's included in the contract.

Book six to eight months in advance; many good musicians are booked a year or more in advance.

Expect to make a deposit when you sign the contract (book the musician).

Ensure the contract specifies that a part of your deposit money will be returned to you if you cancel for any reason.

Ask if the band carries insurance, and if so, what its coverage and liability is.

If the band is not local, verify whether you will be expected to pay for transportation and lodging fees.

Hiring one orchestra to play for cocktails, dinner, and dancing that plays or a DJ who can spin a variety of musical styles.

Book a local band or DJ, so you don't have to pay transportation and/or lodging expenses.

Have a non-continuous contract (one where the musicians break every hour) or have them play after dinner for fewer hours.

Plan an informal wedding for which a smaller group is appropriate, for example, a wedding breakfast, tea, or cocktail reception.

as little as an hour, bands and DJs typically are expected to play for four or five hours with breaks. In the traditional Western wedding scenario, the purpose of the wedding band is to provide music to dance by. Since weddings are typically attended by all ages of people, it's very important that the wedding band plays a variety of music and dance pieces so no one feels left out of the party. However, a really excellent group with a more limited repertoire that almost anyone can enjoy, such as music from the big band era or rhythm and blues, is another good choice.

Often, bandleaders and DJs play the role of announcer during the reception. An experienced band leader or DJ will have an expert sense of timing, not only for music but also for announcing the customary reception highlights, such as the bride and groom's first dance together, the toast, the cutting of the cake, and so on.

If you are not musically inclined, ask the musicians for suggestions. Professional musicians can choose from huge repertoires, sight-read from music sheets, or, with plenty of advance notice, can learn the music of your choice.

For a unique touch, consider booking other forms of entertainment for your event. If you are inviting children, hire a clown to entertain them with skits, makeup, balloon sculptures. Magicians and jugglers can help create magical moments for adults and youngsters alike, and are a wonderful adjunct to medieval-theme weddings.

One way to make your wedding special is to choose music and entertainment that creates an atmosphere appropriate for the occasion. For example, you may want solemn but joyous music for the ceremony and more popular, upbeat music for your reception. Or, you both may be ardent fans of jazz, and want to use jazz throughout your special event. In that case, you might want a vocalist for the ceremony, a pianist for cocktails, and a big band for the reception that all are proficient in some aspect of the jazz tradition. Use the worksheet below to brainstorm your ideas and jot down a ballpark estimate of how you will divide your entertainment dollars

TYPE OF ACT	ESTIMATED COST	NOTES
Rehearsal Dinner		
Ceremony		
Cocktail Party		
Reception		
Other (Engagement Party, Bridesmaids' Lunch, Post-Wedding Party)		

This worksheet contains the questions that are critical for you to ask any singer, band, DJ, or other entertainer whom you are considering booking for your wedding. To help prevent misunderstandings, it's important to keep accurate notes as you interview. Once you've collected this information, you will be able to come up with a couple of possible entertainment scenarios.

	ESTIMATE #1	ESTIMATE #2
Type of Event (indicate Ceremony, Reception, etc.)		
Name of Band/ Musician/DJ/ Entertainer/Act		
Agent or Contact Name, Address, and Phone Number		
Web Site Address		
Type of Music Played/ Act Performed		
Number of Members in Group		
Length of Time Group Has Played Together		
Are the Performers I Heard the Ones Likely to Show Up?		
Master of Ceremonies?		

Then, you can hold more detailed conversations with your preferred vendors. Ask them to send you a contract and carefully compare it to your notes to make sure it accurately reflects your verbal discussion. If you have any doubts, ask for a written clarification of the cost or service in question before signing on the dotted line.

ESTIMATE #3	ESTIMATE #4

	ESTIMATE #1	ESTIMATE #2
Transportation Cost		
Lodging Cost		
What Type of Insurance Does the Band Carry?		
Will They Stay Later Than the Contracted Time Period for An Extra Fee?		
Cost per Hour to Play beyond the Time Contracted For		
Cancellation Clause		
Showcase Dates and Locations		
CD		
Recommended By/ How I Found Them		
Dates and Times Available		
Date I Requested the Contract		
Comments		

ESTIMATE #3	ESTIMATE #4

Chapter 3: Ten Months Ahead

Your Personal Best

Monthly Planner

Sunday	Monday	Tuesday	Wednesday	Thursday	Friday	Saturday

Chapter 3: TEN MONTHS AHEAD

Your Personal Best

Every bride is beautiful, or so the saying goes. But who wants to leave her wedding-day looks to chance? Once your wedding plans are underway, and before you have to finalize a myriad of details, take the time to create a personal care plan that will help maintain your energy and boost your looks in the hectic, and sometimes stress-filled months ahead. Read on for suggestions on how to make the most of healthy, gorgeous you!

THIS MONTH'S TO-DO LIST

1. Assess your looks.

2. Set goals for personal improvement.

3. Design a beauty and fitness plan.

4. Practice the art of managing stress.

Many brides worry about how they will look on their wedding day. It's only natural that they want to look and feel as good as they can on that special day. Looking your best on your wedding day can take some effort and planning. After all, the months leading up to your special day will be incredibly busy and probably rather stressful, and lack of time and stress are two of the most common reasons why people don't take care of themselves.

The secret to looking fabulous on your wedding day is to utilize the same skills you do in other areas of your life — business, school, career, sports, even wedding planning — in the beauty arena. You need to do the following:

- Assess your situation
- Set goals and priorities
- Assemble helpful resources
- Create a plan
- Associate the plan with a timeline
- Commit to following your plan faithfully

This exercise isn't about focusing on flaws, but on being the best you can be. Only you should fill out the Personal Improvement Worksheet. The idea is to realistically assess how you see yourself and what areas you are committing to improve in. The worksheet contains columns such as "Method," "Months to Goal," and "Cost" so that you can get a clear picture of what it will take to achieve your goal. Listed under "Attribute," are some of the most common concerns that bride's have listed, but feel free to ignore them or to add your own goals if they are not on the list.

Personal Improvement Worksheet

ATTRIBUTE	SATISFACTION LEVEL	GOAL	METHOD	FREQUENCY	MONTHS TO GOAL	COST
Skin						
Hair (color, texture)						
Weight						
Shape						
Nails						
Teeth						
Feel						
Diet						
Sleep Habits						
Exercise						
Attitude						
Grooming						
Hairstyle						
Makeup						
Other						

You may not have the knowledge you need at this point to fill out the entire worksheet. For example, you may know you want to lose weight, but you may not know which diet is best for you. Or, you may wish to have a skin condition cleared up, but you may not know which method of treatment offers the best prognosis. In such situations, you will need to assemble some experts to help you. Hollywood

celebrities don't hesitate to get help from teams of professionals, and neither should you, if you can afford it.

Keep in mind that personal image consultants often are not cheap. If you're on a tight budget, consider the following resources: library books and videos on fitness and grooming, image consultation and skincare courses offered at community colleges, and students at beauty and dentistry schools who will work with you at the fraction of the cost of a professional.

While assembling your team, it helps to clip pictures from magazines that represent the look or image you'd like to present, so everyone is on the same page — literally. That way you will run less of a risk of telling a hairstylist or makeup person one thing and discovering to your dismay that the person interpreted what you said completely differently.

Many salons and spas offer special packages targeted toward the bride. They typically include a pre-wedding consultation (bring your headpiece), and then the bride returns on or before the wedding day for a massage, manicure, pedicure, hairstyling with headpiece, and wedding makeup application. Some salons or personal image consultants will perform these services at your home for an extra fee.

Salons also offer days of beauty, in-salon bridesmaids' parties, and discounts for a series of treatments that can be taken prior to the wedding.

	SCHEDULED APPOINTMENTS	REASON
DERMATOLOGIST Name: Address: Phone Number:		
NUTRITIONIST Name: Address: Phone Number:		
FITNESS CONSULTANT/ TRAINER Name: Address: Phone Number:		
MAKEUP ARTIST Name: Address: Phone Number:		
HAIRSTYLIST Name: Address: Phone Number:		
DENTIST Name: Address: Phone Number:		
PHYSICIAN Name: Address: Phone Number:		

	SCHEDULED APPOINTMENTS	REASON
MANICURIST Name: Address: Phone Number:		
FACIALIST Name: Address: Phone Number:		
MASSAGE THERAPIST Name: Address: Phone Number:		
COURSE OR WORKSHOP Name: Address: Phone Number:		
OTHER Name: Address: Phone Number:		
OTHER Name: Address: Phone Number:		
OTHER Name: Address: Phone Number:		

Research shows that at any given moment, a majority of American women wish that they could become both slimmer and more shapely. When you are months away from your wedding — the day you want to look better than ever — the desire to lose weight can become even stronger, especially if the stress of planning this important event has caused you to gain a few pounds in the first place.

Programs that can help you to shed pounds sensibly recommend losing weight slowly through lifestyle changes. Even if you have no weight to lose, eating healthfully provides you with the proper food and nutrition to deal with the pressure that planning a wedding adds to your already-busy days.

Before embarking on any weight-loss program, know that extreme dieting and rapid weight loss can lead to gallstones, constipation, muscle cramps, and a host of other ills. The stress of dieting can also exacerbate existing medical problems. That's why it's important to check with your doctor before dieting and to ask assistance from a nutritionist before creating your meal plan.

Many experts suggest that a food plan supplying between 1,000 and 1,400 calories a day offers a safe, acceptable rate of weight loss. But that is a generalization. Caloric needs are different for different people, so, again, recruit an expert to help you tailor a program for you.

Lifestyle Change Checklist

🦋 Get a general physical exam and talk with your doctor before embarking on any exercise or weight loss routine.

🦋 Diet with a partner — your bridesmaids or mom.

🦋 Stock up on pre-measured, prepackaged foods for those days you don't have time to cook.

🦋 Add more greens and vegetables to your diet.

🦋 Drink a minimum of eight glasses of water a day. Some experts recommend you drink up to an ounce of water for every pound you weigh — consult with your doctor or nutritionist.

🦋 Take a cooking class in preparing light and healthy foods.

🦋 Make a list of unhealthy habits you've developed and work on eliminating one of them per month.

🦋 Enlist support from Internet diet support groups and mentors — many will send you a daily motivational e-mail!

🦋 Contact your local Cooperative State Extension Office; many have information programs on selecting nutrient-dense foods.

🦋 Eat protein and vegetables at every meal.

🦋 Get plenty of sleep; sleep deprivation negatively impacts weight loss and mood.

🦋 Keep a food and exercise diary in which you record your daily successes and failures.

🦋 Make a plan in the evening, and organize your food so you will be prepared when you get up in the morning to accomplish your daily goals.

🦋 Add some of your ideas:

_____
_____
_____
_____
_____
_____

how to read food labels

Ignore the labels telling you what percentage of fat a particular food has. The only way to get at the truth is to do the math: multiply the number of total fat grams by the calories per gram (1 gram = 9 calories). Divide the total calories of the serving by the result to figure out what percentage of the serving size is fat. For example, an eight-ounce cup of soup that has 5 grams of fat and 260 calories is 17 percent fat ($5 \times 9 = 45$ divided by $260 = 17$).

With your diet "mentor," work out a healthy, balanced meal plan that will help you reach your goals safely.

	DAY
BREAKFAST	
Protein	
Vegetable	
Carbohydrate	
Dairy	
Fat	
SNACK	
Protein	
Vegetable	
Carbohydrate	
Dairy	
Fat	
LUNCH	
Protein	
Vegetable	
Carbohydrate	
Dairy	
Fat	
SNACK	
Protein	
Vegetable	
Carbohydrate	
Dairy	
Fat	
DINNER	
Protein	
Vegetable	
Carbohydrate	
Dairy	
Fat	

A certified personal trainer — available free or at a reasonable cost from most gyms and YMCAs — can help you work out a safe exercise plan that will help you reach your fitness goals safely.

	DAY
UPPER-BODY EXERCISES	
LOWER-BODY EXERCISES	
ABS	
CARDIO	

Spa services are great for helping you to de-stress. Once you are in the peaceful atmosphere of a spa salon, your everyday stresses and worries disappear. Schedule a service periodically in the months leading up to your wedding if you can; it will help you to maintain a relaxed attitude and a positive mind-set as you negotiate contracts, deal with canceled appointments, soothe difficult relatives, and experience other tension-producing situations.

As with any inquiries about goods or services, word of mouth is always a fine place to start. A recommendation combined with some basic knowledge of what services are provided can help you find the right spa for your needs. Here, to help you prepare, are a few brief definitions of some common spa services:

Aromatherapy: A part of the Shiatsu massage process, includes the use of essential and scented oils.

Dulse scrub: Uses powdered seaweed and water or oil to scrub and exfoliate entire body.

Herbal wrap: Cloth soaked in an herbal solution is wrapped around the body; used to "detoxify" skin.

Hydrotherapy: Air jets and jet sprays are used for underwater body massage.

Lymphatic drainage: Eliminates water retention through a pumping, massaging technique.

Paraffin wax: Heated wax is rubbed over hands, feet, or other areas of the body, smoothing skin.

Reflexology: A form of pressure-point massage typically for the feet, but can be used for hands or ears.

Shiatsu: Japanese pressure-point massage used to stimulate energy.

Swedish massage: Relaxing European massage technique used to ease muscle aches and tension.

Thalassotherapy: Treatments that include any products from the sea—seaweed wraps, sea salt rubs, and so forth.

Vichy shower: Several showerheads that create a pulsating, sprinkler effect.

Makeup and Hairstyle Tips

- Start on a good skin care regime early.
- Ask for a skin analysis and a personalized skin program.
- Meet with makeup artists and hair stylists no later than three months in advance.
- Early on, pre-wedding consultations allow time to make any changes, such as growing out your hair or working to improve the texture of your skin.
- To keep your bridal makeup natural and refined, opt for makeup in shades of apricot and peach.
- Don't schedule a facial immediately before the wedding day; your skin may look irritated.
- Consider a hairstyle with some height in the front, for a touch of drama.
- An upswept hairdo or a style that pulls hair back from the face in a twisted bun exposes the neck, shows the gown, and forms a feminine, classic line. Your face also will be visible in your wedding pictures.

- Highlight eyes by using neutral contour colors around the eye, mascara on the upper and lower lashes.
- On the day of the wedding, check your makeup often for sheen. If you need to reapply, blot your skin with tissue before applying new powder.
- Drink lots of water.
- Get plenty of rest.
- Visit a dermatologist for any problem that needs medical attention.

Chapter 4: NINE MONTHS AHEAD

Personalizing the Reception

Monthly Planner

Sunday	Monday	Tuesday	Wednesday	Thursday	Friday	Saturday

Chapter 4: Nine Months Ahead

Personalizing the Reception

Most wedding professionals you meet, from the banquet hall to the tuxedo store, will try to sell you a "wedding package." Packages offer the vendor convenience and can often save the bridal couple money. But, it is your wedding, and most likely you will want to personalize it somehow. Here are some ways to ensure that your wedding day is truly unique!

This Month's To-Do List

1. Choose a theme.

2. Select table linens.

3. Rent or buy decorations.

4. Select invitations and announcements.

*Y*ou've always imagined your wedding would be special and unique. Yet, everyone you talk to — from the caterer to the officiant — seems to be handing you a script. The reception hall gives you a four- or five-hour package with a start and an end time. The clergyperson hands you a ceremony from which you cannot deviate. The bandleader has a standard playlist. Your grandma embarrasses you with the suggestion that she plans to pass around a moneybag so everyone can pay to dance with you just as they did in the old country when she was a girl.

There are ways to create a lovely wedding that don't fall in lockstep with the established wedding mill. You can get married and honeymoon in the same place. Bermuda and some of the Caribbean islands market these so-called "weddingmoons" as money-saving alternatives to a stateside wedding. Another option is to marry in a historic house, bed-and-breakfast, or historic site or museum. But these choices are not for everybody. These alternative spaces often have limited accommodations for guests, able to fit up to fifty people at the most. And they often require extra staging, such as tents (with heaters, in case the temperature drops), portable dance floors, or even tables and chairs to be rented.

Brides whose guest lists include 75 people or more, or who prefer to get married in a specific town (where they attend church or school, perhaps) or who want to get married during nice weather may find it easiest to engage a local catering facility. Only after the contract is signed and the deposit made does the couple have a minute to wonder how to put the "special" back in the wedding day.

Not to worry. There are plenty of ways you can give your wedding celebration a distinctive ambience, one that reflects the personalities of both bride and groom.

tips for making your wedding unique

• **Choose a theme.** Whether you want a traditional wedding or one that is unconventional, deciding on a theme for your wedding helps you to save time by focusing your attention on specific goals. This allows you to set priorities and skip over inappropriate suggestions or ideas. For example, if you decide upon a country-style wedding, you can immediately eliminate any decorating schemes, including colors, fabrics, flowers, and accessories, that lack that country feeling. Knowing your theme immediately opens you up to flexibility and inspiration, such as using terracotta pots filled with colorful mums to line the church aisle instead of the conventional satin ribbon and floral pew markers.

• **Choose a palette.** Putting a wedding together involves a lot of interior design. Think like a good interior designer, and select a color palette. Choose one main color that is either warm or cool, and a secondary, "accent" color that is the opposite of the first. Warm colors are red, pink, and yellow. Cool colors are blue, green, and sometimes purple. Contrast a warm color with a cool color.

• **Accessorize**. Creative table accents go a long way toward giving your wedding a one-of-a-kind ambience. For example, if the groom is interested in trains, why not work them into the centerpiece?

• **Feature creative entertainment or entertainers.** Spice up the party by including unexpected games or activities that will charm your guests. If you and your intended enjoy golf, arrange for time at the putting green during cocktails.

• **Appreciate your guests with thoughtful gestures.** If the ladies room at your catering hall is less than luxurious, then consider decorating the counter with a beautiful piece of fabric and a gift basket stocked with sample soaps and lotions. This will make your guests feel appreciated, and make your wedding one they'll remember!

Many couples today are holding theme weddings that evoke another era, such as the Middle Ages or the Civil War period. A whole "period wedding" industry has arisen to service these couples, including custom gown designers.

Designer Props

- Silk flower garlands
- Plaster, resin, and plastic columns
- Latticework screens, arbors, and gazebos
- Fountains
- Balloon arches and sculptures
- Handpainted runners for the church aisle
- Doves (live birds to be released during your exit or entrance)
- Decorated birdcages
- Butterflies to be released at the reception
- Frosted plastic bells
- Cut paper lace streamers or punched paper decorations
- White party lights
- Custom table toppers in floral prints, lace, damask, or jacquard, with fabric swags for banquet tables
- Fabric canopies
- Confetti
- Classical urns and statuary
- White heated tents for outdoor receptions
- Silk ficus trees and potted rose topiaries
- Upgraded china, flatware, and glasses
- Toasting goblet for bride and groom
- Candelabra
- Streamers
- Candles: unity candle and tapers for the ceremony; decorative candles in a color to match your reception hall's decor

Decor Worksheet

Supplier Name:		Phone No.:	
Address:		E-mail:	
		Web site:	

ITEM:	DESCRIPTION:	COST:	ORDER DATE:	DEPOSIT:	BALANCE DUE:

Supplier Name:		Phone No.:	
Address:		E-mail:	
		Web site:	

ITEM:	DESCRIPTION:	COST:	ORDER DATE:	DEPOSIT:	BALANCE DUE:

Supplier Name:		Phone No.:	
Address:		E-mail:	
		Web site:	

ITEM:	DESCRIPTION:	COST:	ORDER DATE:	DEPOSIT:	BALANCE DUE:

INVITATIONS AND PLACE CARDS

Paper, script, and ink color reflect your personality and set the tone for your wedding. If your invitation is formal, guests will expect your wedding to be formal. If you send an invitation that has a more colorful and lighthearted feeling, guests will expect that casual spirit to be reflected on your wedding day.

Stationery goods come into play again on your wedding day. Place cards are the traditional means of helping guests to find their assigned seats. Again, these cards, however small, can help personalize your wedding by displaying a decorative motif in keeping with your wedding theme.

MARRIAGE CERTIFICATES

The location of your marriage will decree the look of your official marriage certificate, but as a special commemorative gesture, consider a custom marriage certificate done by a master calligrapher. Another option is a custom marriage ornamented with a decorative cutouts or small strips of paper rolled into decorative effects called quilling.

The custom of the ketubah is surely one of the longest-standing of the ornamental marriage certificates. For 2,000 years, the Hebrew word ketubah has been used to refer to the certificate that Jewish law required to document a wedding. Perhaps the original prenuptial agreement, the ketubah was a legal and financial agreement that spelled out the groom's responsibilities to the bride, establishing and enumerating a financial contract between the parties, including the dowry. But ketubot are more than just matter-of-fact business documents; hand-lettered and decorated with colorful designs, they acknowledge the celebratory aspect of God's commandment.

❧ Compare styles, price ranges and delivery schedules for invitations and other paper goods before making your decision.

❧ Custom invitations ordered from manufacturers have different delivery times — some at four weeks, some at six weeks. Shop early enough so ordering time does not limit your selection.

❧ You can also choose from a smaller range of do-it-yourself invitations from an office supply store. These can be run through your home laser or inkjet printer.

❧ If you have a lot of patience, you can emboss store-bought invitations one-by-one with gold foil.

❧ Invitations consisting of a translucent piece of paper on top of heavier stock fastened at the top with a ribbon are an increasingly popular option. These also can be found in do-it-yourself supply stores.

Mr. and Mrs. Joseph A. ̶
request the honor of your pre̶
at the marriage of their daug̶
Denise Ann
to
Michael Joseph Spatarella
son of Mr. and Mrs. Anthony J. Spatarella
on Saturday, the twenty-third of June
Two thousand and one
at two o'clock in the afternoon
St. Robert Bellarmine Church
3x5 Euclid Avenue
Warrington, Pennsylvania

Engraving was invented in the seventeenth century as an easy way to reproduce documents that monks had formerly penned by hand. An engraver cuts an image in reverse into a copper plate or steel die. The die is then used to impress paper with ink. The resulting type feels sharp to the touch. Today only invitations for the most formal weddings are engraved, traditionally with a simple Roman script on 100% cotton fiber paper.

Thermography was designed to look like engraving. The process uses a paper plate with an aluminum backing to chemically transfer an image of the lettering on paper. Resinous powder is then applied to the wet ink. As heat melts the powder, it sticks to the ink and raises the lettering. The paper itself remains flat. Although it is raised lettering, it is not as sharp as engraving. However, it is much less expensive.

Calligraphy is still hand-penned by artists as it has been for centuries using black or colored ink in copperplate or italic lettering. The fanciest calligraphy styles have additional embellishments, such as hand-painted roses, or ornamental flourishes reminiscent of the folk art.

Chancery-style lettering, similar to that found on the Declaration of Independence, is popular, not just because it is endorsed by tradition, but also because it uses little space.

stationery etiquette

Traditional etiquette decreed it acceptable to include the reception invitation at the bottom of the ceremony invitation, along with the notation, "Please respond." Response cards and a self-addressed, stamped envelope are new customs that have developed over the past couple of decades. Addressing envelopes by hand saves the cost of calligraphy or printing and adds a personal touch to your invitation.

INVITATION WORKSHEET

Supplier Name:		Phone No.:		
Address:		E-mail:		
		Web site:		

ITEM:	DESCRIPTION:	COST:	ORDER DATE:	DEPOSIT:	BALANCE DUE:

Supplier Name:		Phone No.:		
Address:		E-mail:		
		Web site:		

ITEM:	DESCRIPTION:	COST:	ORDER DATE:	DEPOSIT:	BALANCE DUE:

Supplier Name:		Phone No.:		
Address:		E-mail:		
		Web site:		

ITEM:	DESCRIPTION:	COST:	ORDER DATE:	DEPOSIT:	BALANCE DUE:

Chapter 5: Eight Months Ahead

The Bride's Gown (and Other Wedding Attire)

MONTHLY PLANNER

Sunday	Monday	Tuesday	Wednesday	Thursday	Friday	Saturday

Chapter 5: EIGHT MONTHS AHEAD

The Bride's Gown (and Other Wedding Attire)

A bridal gown may be the most expensive dress a woman will ever buy; certainly it will be the most meaningful. In the past, when fashion rules were strict, brides had few options beyond a long white dress. Today, there are few restrictions on what to wear. Here's how to choose a look that will flatter the bride's style, looks, and budget — and those of the groom and attendants, too!

THIS MONTH'S TO-DO LIST

1. Shop for the bridal gown.

2. Shop for wedding party attire.

3. Determine groom's attire.

If you're a typical bride, you probably have already been out looking for the dress of your dreams — in fact, you've probably been designing it off and on for decades!

But choosing a wedding gown isn't all about fantasy; there are some very real issues to consider. Experienced salon professionals will say the most important question a bride should ask is whether she plans to wear a dress, or whether the dress will be wearing her.

Many women are entranced by elaborate wedding gown confectionary, only to realize in retrospect that not every bridal gown style looks good on everyone. If you want to look your best, it pays to know what looks good on you and what doesn't, and to choose your wedding gown accordingly. The dress that looks right is the one that looks right on you.

Although there are trends in wedding gown fashion, they move much more slowly than trends in the rest of the fashion world. A popular wedding gown style may be retained in a designer's line for two or more years. Since most bridal gowns are custom-ordered, a gown that was introduced a few years ago, or one very much like it, may still be available. Additionally, wedding gowns tend to be

more conservative than other clothing styles. Some wedding gown styles never go out of fashion. All of this means that you should have no trouble finding a gown that has the romantic touch you've dreamed of *and* the styling to show off your unique assets.

Tips on Choosing Your Wedding Gown

Consider the season. Although most reception halls have air conditioning and central heating (and with the year-round availability of winter and summer looks), you may be tempted to wear a summer gown in the winter or vice versa. But air conditioning has been known to break in the middle of a reception, and limousines have been known to get flats in the dead of winter. To be on the safe side, look for a gown that is cut in a fabric compatible with the season. For a winter wedding, consider heavy fabrics such as satin, velvet, brocade, taffeta, and moiré. For a summer wedding, choose cotton, silk, linen, batiste, crepe, georgette, and organza.

What about color? Getting married in white is a relatively new tradition. As late as Victorian times, brides dressed in their best, regardless of color. True, diamond-white looks harsh against many complexions. Fortunately, there is a virtual rainbow of whites and off-whites from which to choose.

A contemporary trend has been to manufacture wedding gowns that have some color. Either the entire gown is a pale shade of pink, blue, or taupe, or it contains a contrasting element, such as a blue cummerbund or bow detail, silk flowers or embroidery in pastel shades, even an accent in a dramatic color such as red. If a color looks good on you or makes you feel good, go for it!

Price. Bridal gowns run all prices, but most start at about $1,000. Gowns by celebrity designers often command much higher prices, even if they are simply cut and have no ornamentation. It is perhaps easier to justify the cost of gowns using a large amount of yardage, expensive fabric, such as silk-faced satin, elaborate detailing like hand-applied beading, embroidery, and fine, European laces.

Very inexpensive gowns tend to be made of synthetic materials, such as polyester chiffon, satin, or taffeta. The ornamentation may be glued on rather than sewn on by hand or machine. Seams, in many, although not all, cases may have unfinished edges.

For brides with a modest gown budget, there are options. Discount houses and even fine salons often have sample sales, where dresses in smaller sizes are reduced to less than half-price. A home sewer or expert seamstress can take a small gown and refashion it with inserts if the size is too small. (This should be tried only by someone who can really sew!) Also consider alternatives to the traditional, custom-made wedding gown. A beautiful, white silk suit; a simple, hand-crocheted dress; or a vintage Victorian skirt and blouse would be stunning as well as easier on the budget, with the added benefit of being suitable to wear for other social occasions.

Headpieces. Many gown designers don't make headpieces to match their gowns. A full-service bridal salon can order the same lace that's on your dress and create a headpiece or hat using a purchased form to compliment your gown and hairstyle. Fresh florals or a "jeweled" tiara are other options.

Backs and trains. Since you won't be facing the spectators during most of the ceremony, the back of your gown should have some interesting detail. Traditionally, this was provided by a long train, often ornamented with appliqué lace, silk rosettes, and beading. Three customary lengths for trains are: cathedral (longest), chapel (medium-length), and court (shortest). A Watteau train attaches at the shoulder instead of the waist and is often made of sheer fabric so the bride's figure can be seen in silhouette. Trains are either detachable or can be bustled for dancing.

But the back of your gown does not have to be extravagant to provide interest. A simple bow, single silk flower, clever draping of fabric, panel in a contrasting fabric or color, or a low, V-cut would all be successful alternatives to a traditional train.

Most salons require a deposit of 50% of the cost of your gown at the time you order it and the balance at the first fitting. Alterations are an additional expense. Almost all bridal gowns require some kind of alteration. Ask if the salon has an in-house seamstress to fit the gown to your body and inquire about the cost. Read all contracts carefully, and order well in advance of your wedding to allow for problems in delivery, fitting, and alterations.

Attendants

You can utilize much of the above information when shopping for attendants' dresses. Most brides want their bridesmaids to wear dresses that reflect the same styling as their own. Dressing so many different figures in the same outfit can be a problem, though. You might wish to opt for several different dresses all made in the same color and material.

It is a traditional joke in the wedding industry that most women cannot wear their bridesmaid's dress again. Large floral prints, bright colors, and fussy detailing often distinguish a bridesmaid's dresses from elegant formalwear. Be considerate of your bridesmaids when choosing a color scheme and gown style. Today, it is not unusual for bridesmaids to glide down the aisle garbed in a classic "little black dress." In times past, choosing a cocktail dress for a bridesmaid's dress would have been considered shocking; today many consider it praiseworthy.

Keeping accurate records is critical when shopping for a gown, or when assembling the necessary information to place an order. Our record sheets, on the following pages, provide plenty of room to record critical information from your shopping trips, as well as your final order.

my measurements

Height:

Bust:

Waist:

Hips (7 to 9 inches below waist):

Inseam:

Neck:

Across shoulders:

Neck to waist:

Waist to floor (without shoes):

Dress size:

Arm length (shoulder to wrist):

Upper arm circumference:

Hat size (or circumference of head):

Shoe size:

FIGURE TYPE	CONSIDER
Long, slender neck	High necklines, Victorian styling, tailored neckbands, stand-up collars
Small shoulder	Portrait neckline, cape, Leg-o'mutton sleeves, puffed sleeves, cabbage rosettes on sleeves
Heavy figure	V-shaped neckline, elongated waist; A-line or princess-line dress, tailored suit
Large bust	A sweetheart bodice has a curvy, heart-shape as its name implies and the look is romantic; avoid square and off-the-shoulder necklines, asymmetrical detailing on bodice
Narrow hips	Detailing (lace, ornamentation, horizontal banding) at bottom of skirt, empire waists, full skirts
Slim and tall	Vintage Victorian skirt and blouse, hand-crocheted or all-over beaded dress
Broad shoulders	Strapless gown; halter necklines; bolero jacket; asymmetrical bodice; sleeveless tailored sheath

	GOWN/ITEM STYLE NUMBER/ DESIGNER	DESCRIPTION
GOWN		
HEADPIECE		
UNDERGARMENTS *(petticoat, bras, corsets)*		
ACCESSORIES *(gloves, jackets, scarves)*		
SHOES		
OTHER		

SALON LOCATION/CONTACT NAME/ PHONE NUMBER	COST	ORDERING INFORMATION

	GOWN/ITEM STYLE NUMBER/DESIGNER	DESCRIPTION	SALON LOCATION/CONTACT NAME/PHONE NUMBER
GOWN			
HEADPIECE			
UNDERGARMENTS (petticoat, bras, corsets)			
ACCESSORIES (gloves, jackets, scarves)			
SHOES			
OTHER			

COST	DEPOSIT/DATE	BALANCE DUE	ARRIVAL DATE	FITTING DATE	PICK-UP

Name:		Phone no.:	
Address:		Bridal party member:	
		Coloring/other features:	

MEASUREMENTS

Height:	Neck to waist:
Bust:	Waist to floor *(without shoes)*:
Waist:	Dress size:
Hips *(7" to 9" below waist)*:	Arm length *(shoulder to wrist)*:
Inseam:	Upper arm circumference:
Neck:	Hat size *(or circumference of head)*:
Across shoulders:	Shoe size:

Name:		Phone no.:	
Address:		Bridal party member:	
		Coloring/other features:	

MEASUREMENTS

Height:	Neck to waist:
Bust:	Waist to floor *(without shoes)*:
Waist:	Dress size:
Hips *(7" to 9" below waist)*:	Arm length *(shoulder to wrist)*:
Inseam:	Upper arm circumference:
Neck:	Hat size *(or circumference of head)*:
Across shoulders:	Shoe size:

Name:		Phone no.:	
Address:		Bridal party member:	
		Coloring/other features:	

MEASUREMENTS

Height:		Neck to waist:
Bust:		Waist to floor *(without shoes)*:
Waist:		Dress size:
Hips *(7" to 9" below waist)*:		Arm length *(shoulder to wrist)*:
Inseam:		Upper arm circumference:
Neck:		Hat size *(or circumference of head)*:
Across shoulders:		Shoe size:

Name:		Phone no.:	
Address:		Bridal party member:	
		Coloring/other features:	

MEASUREMENTS

Height:		Neck to waist:
Bust:		Waist to floor *(without shoes)*:
Waist:		Dress size:
Hips *(7" to 9" below waist)*:		Arm length *(shoulder to wrist)*:
Inseam:		Upper arm circumference:
Neck:		Hat size *(or circumference of head)*:
Across shoulders:		Shoe size:

Name:		Phone no.:	
Address:		Bridal party member:	
		Coloring/other features:	

MEASUREMENTS

Height:	Neck to waist:
Bust:	Waist to floor *(without shoes)*:
Waist:	Dress size:
Hips *(7" to 9" below waist)*:	Arm length *(shoulder to wrist)*:
Inseam:	Upper arm circumference:
Neck:	Hat size *(or circumference of head)*:
Across shoulders:	Shoe size:

Name:		Phone no.:	
Address:		Bridal party member:	
		Coloring/other features:	

MEASUREMENTS

Height:	Neck to waist:
Bust:	Waist to floor *(without shoes)*:
Waist:	Dress size:
Hips *(7" to 9" below waist)*:	Arm length *(shoulder to wrist)*:
Inseam:	Upper arm circumference:
Neck:	Hat size *(or circumference of head)*:
Across shoulders:	Shoe size:

Name:		Phone no.:	
Address:		Bridal party member:	
		Coloring/other features:	

MEASUREMENTS

Height:		Neck to waist:	
Bust:		Waist to floor *(without shoes)*:	
Waist:		Dress size:	
Hips *(7" to 9" below waist)*:		Arm length *(shoulder to wrist)*:	
Inseam:		Upper arm circumference:	
Neck:		Hat size *(or circumference of head)*:	
Across shoulders:		Shoe size:	

Name:		Phone no.:	
Address:		Bridal party member:	
		Coloring/other features:	

MEASUREMENTS

Height:		Neck to waist:	
Bust:		Waist to floor *(without shoes)*:	
Waist:		Dress size:	
Hips *(7" to 9" below waist)*:		Arm length *(shoulder to wrist)*:	
Inseam:		Upper arm circumference:	
Neck:		Hat size *(or circumference of head)*:	
Across shoulders:		Shoe size:	

BRIDAL ATTENDANT SHOPPING RECORD SHEET
NAME:

	GOWN/ITEM STYLE NUMBER/DESIGNER	DESCRIPTION	SALON LOCATION/CONTACT NAME/PHONE NUMBER
GOWN			
HEADPIECE			
ACCESSORIES *(gloves, jackets, scarves)*			
SHOES			
OTHER			

COST	DEPOSIT/DATE	BALANCE DUE	ARRIVAL DATE	FITTING	PICK-UP

Bridal Attendant Shopping Record Sheet

Name:

	GOWN/ITEM STYLE NUMBER/DESIGNER	DESCRIPTION	SALON LOCATION/CONTACT NAME/PHONE NUMBER
GOWN			
HEADPIECE			
ACCESSORIES *(gloves, jackets, scarves)*			
SHOES			
OTHER			

COST	DEPOSIT/DATE	BALANCE DUE	ARRIVAL DATE	FITTING	PICK-UP

Bridal Attendant Shopping Record Sheet
Name:

	GOWN/ITEM STYLE NUMBER/DESIGNER	DESCRIPTION	SALON LOCATION/CONTACT NAME/PHONE NUMBER
GOWN			
HEADPIECE			
ACCESSORIES (gloves, jackets, scarves)			
SHOES			
OTHER			

COST	DEPOSIT/DATE	BALANCE DUE	ARRIVAL DATE	FITTING	PICK-UP

NAME:

	GOWN/ITEM STYLE NUMBER/DESIGNER	DESCRIPTION	SALON LOCATION/CONTACT NAME/PHONE NUMBER
GOWN			
HEADPIECE			
ACCESSORIES (gloves, jackets, scarves)			
SHOES			
OTHER			

COST	DEPOSIT/DATE	BALANCE DUE	ARRIVAL DATE	FITTING	PICK-UP

Bridal Attendant Shopping Record Sheet

Name:

	GOWN/ITEM STYLE NUMBER/DESIGNER	DESCRIPTION	SALON LOCATION/CONTACT NAME/PHONE NUMBER
GOWN			
HEADPIECE			
ACCESSORIES *(gloves, jackets, scarves)*			
SHOES			
OTHER			

COST	DEPOSIT/DATE	BALANCE DUE	ARRIVAL DATE	FITTING	PICK-UP

NAME:

	GOWN/ITEM STYLE NUMBER/DESIGNER	DESCRIPTION	SALON LOCATION/CONTACT NAME/PHONE NUMBER
GOWN			
HEADPIECE			
ACCESSORIES (gloves, jackets, scarves)			
SHOES			
OTHER			

COST	DEPOSIT/DATE	BALANCE DUE	ARRIVAL DATE	FITTING	PICK-UP

Bridal Attendant Shopping Record Sheet

Name:

	GOWN/ITEM STYLE NUMBER/DESIGNER	DESCRIPTION	SALON LOCATION/CONTACT NAME/PHONE NUMBER
GOWN			
HEADPIECE			
ACCESSORIES *(gloves, jackets, scarves)*			
SHOES			
OTHER			

COST	DEPOSIT/DATE	BALANCE DUE	ARRIVAL DATE	FITTING	PICK-UP

BRIDAL ATTENDANT SHOPPING RECORD SHEET

NAME:

	GOWN/ITEM STYLE NUMBER/DESIGNER	DESCRIPTION	SALON LOCATION/CONTACT NAME/PHONE NUMBER
GOWN			
HEADPIECE			
ACCESSORIES (gloves, jackets, scarves)			
SHOES			
OTHER			

COST	DEPOSIT/DATE	BALANCE DUE	ARRIVAL DATE	FITTING	PICK-UP

THE GROOM

The groom has the responsibility of taking care of his own attire and that of his attendants. But, naturally, a bride will want some say in the color, cut, and look of the male wedding party's attire. Although the men's attire does not have to be ordered as far in advance as the women's, mostly because it is typically rented or purchased off the rack, it's smart to discuss appropriate options for your wedding style well in advance.

TRADITIONAL WEDDING WEAR FOR GROOMS AND USHERS

Formal: A traditional full-dress tuxedo or tailcoat.

Morning weddings: The cutaway, also known as a morning suit, has a dark gray coat, worn buttoned in front, which curves away gradually to tailcoat-length in back.

Semi-formal: Tuxedos with short coats, which can be either waist- or suit-length, either single- or double-breasted.

Casual: Navy blue blazer with white shirt, red patterned tie or bowtie, and camel or gray trousers.

Colors: Black endures as the favorite color, but gray is increasingly worn for daytime, especially a deeper gray jacket paired with lighter gray pants. In summer, look for white, ivory, or one of the new silver shades. Shadow stripes and textural weaves are a contemporary trend in all colors. Traditionally, the groom's cummerbund is color-coordinated with either the satin of his lapel or the bride's gown. Ushers' cummerbunds are often matched to the color of the bridesmaids' dresses.

Fabrics: The most popular fabrics are still wool and silk (in weights appropriate for the season) but the trendy groom could also opt for rayon.

Shirts: A white pleated shirt with ascot or winged collar and bow tie.

Shoes: Shiny, plain-toe tied shoes, slip-ons, or kiltie styles in black, white or silver.

Chapter 6: SEVEN MONTHS AHEAD

Flowers, Cakes, and Other Embellishments

MONTHLY PLANNER

Sunday	Monday	Tuesday	Wednesday	Thursday	Friday	Saturday

Chapter 6: SEVEN MONTHS AHEAD

Flowers, Cakes, and Other Embellishments

Flowers, wedding cake, and champagne are traditional accompaniments to the wedding feast, lending a romantic and celebratory air to the marital celebration.

THIS MONTH'S TO-DO LIST

1. Engage a florist.

2. Shop for wedding cake.

3. Select sweets.

4. Shop for favors.

5. Champagne toasts.

Today, elegant embellishments have reached new heights of fancy. Flowers that once were available only in season are now flown in from out of the country during off seasons, and new hybrids have been developed in what are considered to be more romantic or prettier colors. Floral designers are at their most creative today — utilizing both classic forms and unusual contemporary ones. Cake designers, too, have rediscovered techniques from the past and invented new ones as well. Old customs, such as the dessert table, are being revived, while new ones, such as the groom's cake, are being invented. Unusual choices or classic tradition can contribute to making your wedding banquet truly a pièce de résistance!

In Victorian times brides carried bou-
quets of flowers chosen for their symbolic meanings. Many of those flowers,
such as roses, lilies of the valley, orchids,
and stephanotis, are still popular today
and express the traditional sentiments.
The traditional bridal bouquet was
white. Today's bride, however, can
choose from a wider selection of exotic
flowers and colors (some natural and
some artificially enhanced) offering varied colors and longevity.

Most flowers are available year-
round since they are imported from all
over the world, including Holland,
South America, and Africa. Although
ordering flowers from foreign countries
will not drastically increase the price,
florists say that locally grown flowers are less expensive. Roses may cost more during hol-
idays, especially Valentine's Day. Ordering flowers in season, such as tulips and hyacinths
in spring, may be a frugal, appropriate choice.

Florists typically advise against some varieties of flowers. For example, lilies of the valley are very fragile and short-lived and can be very expensive to order not to mention
unavailable out of season. Other flowers of short duration include gardenias, anemones,
and daffodils. In addition to not being long lasting, dahlias are rarely used because they
are so large.

Just as every wedding will have its own theme based on a color scheme or mood, the
choice of flowers will reflect individual tastes. Although there are no hard and fast rules,
combinations of different flowers can enhance the wedding's theme. For country style, try
anemones, baby's breath, field daisies, gerbera daisies, heather, irises, or miniature carna-
tions. For an exotic, modern look, try calla lilies, or irises. For a formal or traditional
wedding, try chrysanthemums, delphiniums, freesias, gardenias, larkspur, orchids,
peonies, roses, and stephanotis. For an English cottage garden feeling, try alstroemerias,
baby's breath, daffodils, delphiniums, freesias, gerbera daisies, hyacinths, lilacs, lilies,
sweet peas, and tulips.

FLOWERS	COLORS	AVAILABILITY	PRICE RANGE	STYLE
Alstroemeria	Yellow, Pink, Red, Orange, Mauve	May to June	Middle	Garden
Anemones	Red, Mauve, Blue, Purple, White	Year-round	Middle or High	Country
Baby's Breath	White	Year-round	Inexpensive	Garden or Country
Calla Lilly	White	March to June	Most Expensive	Exotic or Contemporary
Carnation	Yellow, Pink, Red, Orange, Mauve, White	Year-round	Inexpensive	Country
Chrysanthemum	Yellow, Pink, Red, Orange, Mauve, White	Year-round	Inexpensive	Traditional
Daffodil	Yellow, Yellow-Orange	Year-round	Inexpensive	Garden
Delphinium	Blue, Mauve, Pink, White	Year-round	Middle	Garden or Formal
Field Daisy	White	Year-round	Inexpensive	Garden or Formal
Freesia	Yellow, Pink, Red, Orange, White, Cream	Year-round	Middle	Garden or Formal
Gardenia	White	Year-round	Most Expensive	Formal or Traditional

FLOWERS	COLORS	AVAILABILITY	PRICE RANGE	STYLE
Heather	White	November to March	Middle	Country
Iris	Blue, Mauve, Pink, White, Yellow	March to May	Low or Middle	Country or Contemporary
Lilac	Purple, White	February to May	Middle to High	Garden
Lily	Yellow, Pink, Red, Orange	Year-round	Most Expensive	Exotic or Garden
Lily of the Valley	White	May	Middle to High	Exotic
Orchids	White, Reddish	Year-round	Most Expensive	Formal or Contemporary
Peony	Yellow, Pink, Red, Orange, Mauve	March to May	Middle to High	Traditional
Rose	Yellow, Pink, Red, Orange, Mauve, Yellow	Year-round	Middle to High	Formal or Traditional
Stephanotis	White	Year-round	Most Expensive	Formal or Traditional
Sweet Pea	Pink, Red, Mauve, White	March to May	Middle to High	Garden
Tulip	Yellow, Pink, Red, Yellow	January to May	Inexpensive	Garden

bouquet shapes and options

Round: Classic simplicity, good for smaller brides, works with any wedding look, from country to Victorian

Crescent: Structured half-moon, a more individualistic shape for a bride who wants something different

Basket: Favorite for country or Victorian-style weddings and flower girls

Cascade: Best for grand occasions and statuesque women who can carry it off (think Princess Diana)

Single Flower: Denotes innocence

Wreath: An unusual shape that can evoke the country or Celtic fairy lore

Tussy-mussy: Decorative holder popular in Victorian and Edwardian times, designed to hold flowers in a structured bouquet so the bride's gloved hand would not get soiled.

Bible with Floral Spray: An old tradition, a white bible with floral spray or large orchid attached lends a note of religiosity to the ceremony.

Ceremony Flowers	Type	Budget
Pew decorations		
Runner		
Chuppah/altar flowers		
Bride's bouquet		
Bridesmaids' bouquet(s)		
Flower girl		
Bride's mother's flowers		
Groom's mother's flowers		
Groom's boutonniere		
Usher boutonnieres		
Father of the bride boutonniere		
Father of the groom boutonniere		
Ringbearer boutonniere		
Other (for example, grandparents)		
Reception Flowers		
Centerpieces		
Bride's table		
Occasional arrangements		
Props (columns, screens, lattice, etc.)		
Other (For example, transportation, rest rooms)		

FLORAL BID WORKSHEET

As you comparison shop, record bids you receive below. Photocopy the worksheet if you need more pages and keep in the tab pocket.

Florist Name:		Phone No.:	
Address:		E-mail:	
		Web site:	

BID #:	APPROACH/STYLE:	COMMENTS:	COST:

Florist Name:		Phone No.:	
Address:		E-mail:	
		Web site:	

BID #:	APPROACH/STYLE:	COMMENTS:	COST:

Florist Name:		Phone No.:	
Address:		E-mail:	
		Web site:	

BID #:	APPROACH/STYLE:	COMMENTS:	COST:

The highlight of the wedding banquet is the wedding cake. Traditionally, it is wheeled out to the center of the dance floor on a cart covered with a ruffled skirt. The bride and groom are invited to cut the cake, and they feed each other a small piece. Then the cake is whisked away behind the scenes, to be cut up into individual pieces that are then brought to the guests seated at their tables. Pieces of wedding cake are boxed for guests to take home and slip under their pillows to inspire dreams of love and romance. Traditionally, the top layer of the cake is removed and saved for the couple to enjoy at their first anniversary celebration.

The earliest wedding cakes were piles of buns presented as offerings to ensure a bride's fertility. The traditional wedding cake, however, with its tiers festooned with butter cream swags, dates back to the court of Marie Antoinette. The royal pastry chef, Karame, longed to be an architect, but ended up as cook. He used his passion for architecture to create elaborate castles and palaces of sugar, and the traditional modern wedding cake was born.

Today there are many cake artists who can create equally magnificent creations in flour and sugar. However, many of these are freelance cake "couturiers" that operate away from corner bakeries. If you are interested in something special, perhaps a shape associ-

ated with an interest you both share, you may have to hunt around to find someone who has studied the fine art of cake architecture and decorating.

Do-it-yourselfers can find materials for creating fancy cakes, including molds and plastic architectural embellishments, such as sweeping staircases and gazebos, at any major arts-and-crafts store.

Popular cake toppers include a plastic or porcelain collectible bride and groom, wedding bells, a gazebo, a bouquet of sugar or fresh flowers, an antique cake topper (today, these are highly prized collectibles), or something meaningful to the couple's hobbies.

Cake Decorations

The traditional wedding cake is covered with white icing. Many contemporary couples opt for something with a splash of color. There is no end to possible materials and methods to decorating a wedding cake. Consider this list of possibilities:

- Bas-relief work (three-dimensional decorative elements) created from sugar
- Silicone putty to make imprints of architectural features on a structure, such as moldings, which in turn can be used to make a cake mold to create these features on a cake
- Fresh floral garlands
- Assorted candies
- Icing woven in a basket-weave style
- Plastic enhancements, such as columns, cherubs, staircases, gazebos
- Smooth fondant icing
- Sugar pears
- Silvered confectionary beads
- Handmade porcelain-like sugar roses

Cake Flavors

Traditionally, weddings have one cake for the bride (*the* wedding cake) and one for the groom. The traditional wedding cake comes in three basic flavors: white, yellow pound, or fruitcake, while the groom's cake was a fruitcake. Today's palates are more sophisticated, and many couples opt for chocolate, carrot, red velvet cakes, or just about any other flavor that makes them feel good. Fruit fillings, such as raspberry or apricot jam, applied between cake layers, also are popular.

CAKE BID WORKSHEET

As you comparison shop, record bids you receive below.

Bakery Name:		Phone No.:	
Address:		E-mail:	
		Web site:	

STYLE	SIZE	CAKE TYPE	FILLING	FROSTING	DECORATION	COST	ORDER DATE	DEPOSIT	BALANCE DUE

Bakery Name:		Phone No.:	
Address:		E-mail:	
		Web site:	

STYLE	SIZE	CAKE TYPE	FILLING	FROSTING	DECORATION	COST	ORDER DATE	DEPOSIT	BALANCE DUE

Bakery Name:		Phone No.:	
Address:		E-mail:	
		Web site:	

STYLE	SIZE	CAKE TYPE	FILLING	FROSTING	DECORATION	COST	ORDER DATE	DEPOSIT	BALANCE DUE

A Viennese pastry table is the perfect conclusion to an elegant wedding. Just as the party starts to wind down, and guests brace themselves for departure, out comes the culinary grand finale: a tiered banquet table festooned with draperies, floral garlands, and perhaps an ice sculpture, upon which is displayed a vast selection of pastries, confections, fresh fruits, mousses, and creams served with coffee and liqueurs. Divine!

More than just a dessert buffet, the Viennese table is a complete course in itself. Offered either in place of a served dessert, or as an added course before the end of the reception, the Viennese table presents a grand selection of pastries and confections served with fresh fruits, mousses, creams and liqueurs.

Guests choose their sweets from a table stylishly decorated with flowers, candles or ice sculpture. Used as a dessert buffet, the Viennese table acts to bring back the party atmosphere after a filling dinner.

Served after the closing of the bar, the Viennese table also provides the added benefit of allowing guests who have been drinking to prepare for the drive home.

While almost any kind of sweet can be used, most Viennese tables consist of a number of mini-pastries popular in Austria. Miniature éclairs, napoleons, and assorted miniature cream puffs are favorites. Classic tortes, cakes rich with eggs, butter and a variety of fillings in which ground nuts take the place of flour, are mainstay. The jam-filled linzer and chocolate Sacher tortes often top the list. Fresh fruit, flavored mousses, and fruit tarts are also very popular, and cordials and an international coffee bar are often included. As additions, crepes, desserts flambé, or fondues are also available through some caterers. Coffees and cordials or liqueurs (often served in miniature chocolate cups), accompany this sugar spectacular.

In addition to sugar, the unifying theme of the presentation is miniaturization, so guests can sample an array of sweet tidbits.

Grand though the traditional pastry table is in itself, some contemporary caterers feel they have to add a unique, theatrical edge to the final moment, and so more extreme additions to the presentation of this course are occasionally offered, such as dancing waiters with sparklers.

While some caterers offer prearranged packages that include a Viennese table with the reception, many others will create a custom selection based on the couple's preference and charge an additional Viennese table fee per guest, on top of the package price for the wedding reception.

- Miniature Austrian or French pastry
- Black forest cake
- Linzer torte
- Sacher torte
- Assorted cheese cakes
- Cream puffs
- Fruited custard cups
- Carved fruit display
- Lemon pound cake covered with fondant
- Orange poppyseed cake flavored with caramel buttercream
- Linzer cookies
- Petit fours
- Sicilian cannoli filled with cream or ricotta and chocolate chips
- Fruit tarts
- Cannoli
- Éclairs
- Italian cookies
- Chocolate-chip cookies
- White and dark chocolate mousse served in edible chocolate cups
- Fresh strawberries with melted dipping chocolate
- Assorted fresh fruits with sweet dipping sauces
- Chocolate candies
- Nuts
- Coffee bar
- Cordials served in miniature chocolate goblets
- Fresh flowers
- Ice sculpture
- Flambé station
- Fruit fondue
- Raspberry truffle
- Mixed-nut tarts
- Lemon bars

- Red-wine poached pears with vanilla sauce
- Cream horns
- Napoleons
- Cream puffs
- Fruited custard cups
- Éclairs
- Chocolate or mint candy coffee stirrers
- Gold-banded coffee cups and plates
- Flatware, including teaspoons dipped in chocolate
- Candelabra
- Cost per person $_____

CHAMPAGNE

A highlight of the wedding reception is the champagne toast, proposed by the best man to the bride, first, and then to the groom, with others joining in — the bride to her parents, the groom to his, and so on.

Included with many banquet hall reception fees is the cost of the champagne toast (or, more accurately, the sparkling wine toast, for many caterers typically serve champagne-like beverages that do not come directly from the Champagne region in France).

Small bottles of champagne or sparkling wine, adorned with custom labels bearing the couple's name and wedding date and perhaps a white satin bow, are popular wedding favors. Where local vineyards are plentiful, couples may gift guests with small bottles of local wine. Check with local laws; in some states (and hotels), you cannot bring cases of alcohol purchased from an outside vendor into a reception or banquet hall and in others you can bring the small bottles in as long as they remain unstoppered or are contained in sealed bags and distributed at the end of the evening as favors.

CIGARS

Cigars play center stage at many contemporary bachelor parties and have a presence at many sophisticated urban weddings. A suitable gift for a groom, father-of-the bride, or usher who is a cigar aficionado might be a silver cigar cutter engraved with the couple's name and wedding date, along with some handcrafted cigars. Cigar cases, which hold three to four cigars and fit inside a man's jacket pocket, are another thoughtful wedding favor.

For a touch of sophistication, consider finishing an evening reception by offering guests a cigar with cognac. Place a small box of eight cigars at each table of ten guests and invite guests to try the cigars after dinner at 9 p.m., with a coffee bar.

Many reception establishments may not allow cigars to be smoked or may only allow them in certain rooms with sophisticated air-filtration equipment. Cigars can then be offered to guests as wedding favors to be enjoyed later.

If you choose to purchase cigars in advance, keep in mind that a temperature of 70 degrees with 70-percent humidity is the perfect atmosphere for preserving a fine cigar.

The modern wedding often includes the tradition of giving each guest a wedding memento engraved, stamped, or printed with the couple's name and the wedding date. People have become ever-more inventive in designing favors in keeping with their personal interests or wedding theme. Here are just a few ideas.

- Small bottles of custom-labeled wine or champagne
- Matchbooks or boxes
- Sugared almonds tied in tulle with a ribbon printed with the name and date
- Goody bags filled with interesting soaps and perfumes (for women) or soaps and colognes (for men).
- Silver-plated picture frames with the guest's name and table number printed on a card that can later be removed and substituted with the couple's photo.
- Monogrammed glasses
- Small baskets filled with candy
- Molded chocolate sculpture
- Heart-shaped cookies in decorative envelope bags
- Disposable cameras
- Small photo albums

Chapter 7: SIX MONTHS AHEAD

Guests and Gifts

Monthly Planner

Sunday	Monday	Tuesday	Wednesday	Thursday	Friday	Saturday

Chapter 7: SIX MONTHS AHEAD

Guests and Gifts

A wedding is more than a commitment between two people, it's also a public commitment made to the community, and before witnesses. Now is the time to decide who is special enough to be invited to share your joy, and how to do the actual inviting. Is a stepparent in the picture? Does a family member insist someone be invited, while another family member insists they'd rather not? This month's focus is on how to negotiate such tricky social waters and in general explains how to be a gracious hostess to all involved.

THIS MONTH'S TO-DO LIST

1. Assemble guest lists.

2. Plan a bridesmaids' lunch.

3. Register for gifts.

Deciding whom to invite to your wedding often takes a lot of diplomacy. There are friends, relatives, and sometimes, even business acquaintances to consider when preparing your guest list. Perhaps you find yourself in the unfortunate position of being caught in the middle of a parent's divorce or having to deal with unpleasant family politics. (It can happen in the best families.) Money is often a consideration. You may not have the budget to invite everyone, and, even if you do, inviting the whole office may seem a bit over-the-top if you truly are not close to everyone.

It is important to remember that your wedding is *your* day. You and your groom are the ones who will live with your guest list for years to come. In the end, who is and who isn't invited is up to you. Listen to your hearts, be somewhat practical, and make up your list accordingly.

The Guest List Organizer , in the next few pages, was designed to keep track of your wedding guests and the parties to which they are invited. Note — your wedding guests are not just the people who are invited to the wedding banquet. There are a number of social events that happen during the course of planning a wedding, and you will want to keep track of who comes to these smaller parties, too.

In days past, etiquette spelled out who threw which of these events, and who was permitted to attend. You can consult an etiquette book for the traditional point of view on who should throw what party and who should be invited to what affair. In the past, for example, the parents threw the engagement party, the bride never attended the stag party, and so on. Today, however, many of these traditional boundaries have faded a bit. Many brides throw their own bridal showers, while others have attended the stag party. Is it proper? I suppose it depends on the circles you travel in, how individualistic and modern you are, and the nuances of what passes for acceptable behavior in your own select circle of friends.

You may decide to skip some of the customary parties associated with a wedding. That's fine. But, for those who are preparing a wedding with traditional fanfare, we've provided columns on the worksheet for the most common parties held during the year-long wedding-planning process. Enter a check in the box if you expect to invite that person to one of those events or if someone else throws a party in your honor and invites that person. Even if you do not do the inviting and preparation for that specific party, it helps to keep track of who attended. Naturally you will want to thank them for attending any event held in your honor and for any gift they might give you. You also can cross-reference your parties to ensure that you do not overlook anyone who attended one party when you are compiling guest lists for another party.

On the Guest List Organizer, the day of the big event is color-coded. In these columns, you can indicate whether the person was invited to the reception and ceremony or the ceremony only, and whether they have accepted or regretted your invitations.

guest list organizer key

Guest #: Keeps track of how many people you are considering inviting to a wedding event.

B/G/O: In the "Relationship" column, circle the letter that applies to the guest's relationship to you and your fiancé. Is this person a relative of the bride? Circle B. Is it a friend of the groom? Circle G. Is the person attending neither a friend nor a family member? Circle O for other. For example, a wedding planner, the officiant, or members of the band may all be expected to eat something at the reception and therefore need to be included in your head count.

EP: Engagement Party

BL: Bridesmaid's Lunch

BS: Bridal Shower

OTG: Out-of-town-guests reception

B/BP: Bachelor (a.k.a. Stag) or Bachelorette Party

RD: Rehearsal Dinner

C: Ceremony

R: Reception

ARB: After-reception home reception at a parent's house or next-day-brunch

OH: Open House (newlywed housewarming or parents' open house, either before or after the wedding.)

Your Guest List Organizer

GUEST #	NAME	RELATIONSHIP G/B/O	ADDRESS	PHONE NUMBER
1				
2				
3				
4				
5				
6				
7				
8				
9				
10				
11				
12				
13				
14				
15				
16				
17				
18				
19				
20				
21				
22				
23				
24				
25				
26				
27				
28				
29				
30				
31				
32				

EP	BL	BS	OTG	B/BP	RD	C	R	ACCEPT	REGRET	ARB	OH

Your Guest List Organizer

GUEST #	NAME	RELATIONSHIP G/B/O	ADDRESS	PHONE NUMBER
33				
34				
35				
36				
37				
38				
39				
40				
41				
42				
43				
44				
45				
46				
47				
48				
49				
50				
51				
52				
53				
54				
55				
56				
57				
58				
59				
60				
61				
62				
63				
64				

EP	BL	BS	OTG	B/BP	RD	C	R	ACCEPT	REGRET	ARB	OH

GUEST #	NAME	RELATIONSHIP G/B/O	ADDRESS	PHONE NUMBER
65				
66				
67				
68				
69				
70				
71				
72				
73				
74				
75				
76				
77				
78				
79				
80				
81				
82				
83				
84				
85				
86				
87				
88				
89				
90				
91				
92				
93				
94				
95				
96				

EP	BL	BS	OTG	B/BP	RD	C	R	ACCEPT	REGRET	ARB	OH

YOUR GUEST LIST ORGANIZER

GUEST #	NAME	RELATIONSHIP G/B/O	ADDRESS	PHONE NUMBER
97				
98				
99				
100				
101				
102				
103				
104				
105				
106				
107				
108				
109				
110				
111				
112				
113				
114				
115				
116				
117				
118				
119				
120				
121				
122				
123				
124				
125				
126				
127				
128				

EP	BL	BS	OTG	B/BP	RD	C	R	ACCEPT	REGRET	ARB	OH

GUEST #	NAME	RELATIONSHIP G/B/O	ADDRESS	PHONE NUMBER
129				
130				
131				
132				
133				
134				
135				
136				
137				
138				
139				
140				
141				
142				
143				
144				
145				
146				
147				
148				
149				
150				
151				
152				
153				
154				
155				
156				
157				
158				
159				
160				

EP	BL	BS	OTG	B/BP	RD	C	R	ACCEPT	REGRET	ARB	OH

The wedding day is still far away, so it may seem early to be planning a special pre-wedding thank-you party for your female friends. But time will fly by quickly in the final days leading up to the wedding, so now is the time to make plans for a future get-together with the girls. At the party, you will probably want to thank your friends for all of their help with the wedding plans. You might also want to show your appreciation for their friendship over the years and spend some time reminiscing about your days as single girls. Perhaps you'll recall summers spent together, or times when your friends provided you with much needed comfort Certainly, you'll want to reassure them that their friendship will continue to be important to you. Often, newly married couples go through lifestyle changes that reduce the amount of time they have available for friends. This very personal thank-you party will be the happy occasion that they will remember with much fondness during the early days of your new marriage, when you may not be able to see them as much as you used to.

Your personal thank-you party can take any number of forms — a tea party thrown in your home, a barbecue on the back porch, or a day at the salon (you might want to ask for a group discount). Whatever form it takes, make sure there's plenty of time to talk, laugh, and share your stories. You'll need to bank some sharing against the hectic days ahead!

Gifts That Say Thanks

FOR WOMEN:

- Classic jewelry
- Fancy photo frame
- Photo album
- Diary or journal
- Gift book
- Gift certificate to spa or beautician
- Spa goods
- Lingerie
- Perfume
- Scented candles
- Potpourri scent dispenser
- Custom basket
- Accessory (shawl or bag)
- Tea cup, saucer, small pot
  with assorted tea bags
- Silk, dried, or fresh floral arrangement
- Theatre, concert, or movie tickets
- Decorative gift box
- Music CD
- Fine stationery

The traditional place to register for gifts was a department or jewelry store. Times have changed. Now, most chain stores, including specialty stores, as well as furniture, home centers, travel agencies, and mail-order catalogues offer a bridal registry.

If you opt for a department store or other walk-in retailer, you may be surprised at the efficiency with which your registry is recorded, thanks to modern technology. You will meet with a wedding consultant who will record your information in a computer. You will be handed a gun to use for scanning the product numbers off the merchandise as you walk around the store. The information stored in the scanning gun will be uploaded to the store's computer in a matter of seconds. When your guests come in to buy a gift for you, they will be handed a computer printout. Once they have selected a gift, it will be deleted from the list of items listed in the respective category. For example a printout may show that you asked for four wineglasses in a certain pattern. If a guest purchases all four of them for you, and another guest arrives a day later, the second guest will discover that the item has been taken care of and will be encouraged to buy something for you from the remaining items on your registry list.

Should you register? Registering for gifts is a time-honored tradition, yet many people feel a bit funny about registering. If you don't register, chances are you will receive either duplicates of items or items that do not suit your needs or style. If you and your groom are more established, or you have been married before, you may feel uncomfortable about registering. Many people get around this by asking people to donate money to a charity in the name of a deceased parent, friend, or relative.

Most bridal registrars recommend scheduling two appointments at the beginning, because walking the floor, as they call it, can take from one to three hours. Be considerate of your guests' varied financial situations. Choose a variety of items in different price ranges, so everytone will be able to find something that's in line with what they want to spend. Once you've registered, count on Mom or Sis to convey the whereabouts of your list to the appropriate parties.

Common Wedding Registry Items

- Crystal vases and bowls
- Fine china
- Sterling silver flatware
- Small appliances, such as blenders and toasters
- Table linens
- Kitchen towels and utensils
- Bedroom and bath linens
- Clocks
- Luggage

Before you register, you may wish to do some research on designs and manufacturers. For example, as you visit stores or page through magazines, jot down the names of several china patterns that catch your eye. If a couple of people tell you what their favorite

CATEGORY	MODEL/PATTERN NUMBER	DESCRIPTION	PRICING/BENEFITS
KITCHEN			
BATHROOM			

blender is, record the brand names below. Then, when you do register, you will have a good idea in advance which items will suit your needs best, last the longest, and offer the best value.

CATEGORY	MODEL/PATTERN NUMBER	DESCRIPTION	PRICING/BENEFITS
BEDROOM			
YARD/LANDSCAPE			
OTHER			

Chapter 8: FIVE MONTHS AHEAD

Your Romantic Getaway

The honeymoon is a special time when couples get to know each other all over again in a new context —
as husband and wife. Naturally, you want your travel plans to go as smoothly as possible, so you and
your intended can focus your energies on each other. Plan now for a stress-free honeymoon by utilizing
these tips and suggestions.

THIS MONTH'S TO-DO LIST

1. Book a honeymoon.

2. Learn to pack.

3. Obtain a passport or visa.

4. Attend to legal matters.

To follow your dream wedding with a dream honeymoon, start planning early. As
is the case with reception halls at popular times of the year, popular honeymoon
locales are booked well in advance, too.

If you are planning a trip to another country, you may find that the date and time
of your trip does not coincide with the end of your wedding reception. You will need
to plan what to do during this "lag" time. Many couples book a room at an airport
hotel, only to find it is one of the least romantic places to spend the wedding night,
with planes taking off overhead every few minutes.

To avoid this, it might be a good idea to plan to take off for your honeymoon one or two days after the wedding. The intervening time can be spent at a small bed-and-breakfast, cabin in the woods, at a romantic weekend getaway, or simply holed up in your new house (decorated, cleaned, and well-stocked with gourmet nibbles ahead of time).

Next, discuss with your partner what type of honeymoon you would both enjoy most. This may take some negotiating skills, since it's very rare for two people to have exactly the same tastes! You may like antiquing and visiting museums, while he or she may prefer a bike ride through the countryside. Many travel destinations offer a variety of experiences, and you can take advantage of this fact if you know what your priorities are and plan carefully from the start.

The type of trip you choose will also depend on how comfortable you feel traveling to unfamiliar destinations by yourself. If you are planning a trip in an unfamiliar place, don't speak the native language, or are on a strict budget, you may prefer an all-inclusive resort, tour, or cruise with a package price. Booking early often means getting a discount. Also check out deals offered by airlines and travel companies.

Brainstorming Your Honeymoon Location

Ask yourself the following questions before you start researching your "trip of a lifetime."

- What are your interests and hobbies (list)?
- What food do you like to eat?
- Are you physically fit? Can you walk long distances?
  Do you prefer to get physical exercise every day?
- Are you interested in learning more about a particular culture?
- During what time of year will you travel?
- How important is temperature and weather to you?
- Do you speak the language of another country sufficiently well
  enough to go it alone?
- Have you traveled extensively prior to your honeymoon?
- How much money can you afford to spend on your honeymoon?

Once you estimate the total dollar cost you plan to budget for your honeymoon, you can get down to specifics. To get a good idea of how much your dream honeymoon might cost, fill out the worksheet below.

TRANSPORTATION	
Car:	
Airfare:	
Train:	
Taxi:	
Tips:	
Subway:	
Other:	

HOTEL/LODGING	
No. of nights x	
rate per night:	
Taxes and tips:	
Phone/fax/video fees:	
Housekeeping extras:	

FOOD/DINING	
Number of meals per day x	
average cost per meal:	
Drinks:	
Gratuity:	

ENTERTAINMENT	
Sightseeing	
Shopping	
Sports	
Theater	
Museums	
Bus fare	
Cloakroom fees	
Salons and spas	
Amusement parks	
Boat rides	
Beach fees	
Day excursions	
Personal sundries	
Clotheswashing/laundry	
Travel insurance	
Film	
Reading matter	
Other:	
TOTAL COST:	

Travel Documents Checklist

- Airline tickets
- Passport
- Visas (if needed for your destination)
- Driver's license
- Marriage license
- Copy of birth certificate (certified)
- Proof of inoculations (if necessary; check for government advisories on the Department of State Web site)
- Itinerary
- Emergency phone numbers (if going abroad, check with U.S. State Department for a list of helpful numbers to contact in case of an emergency)
- Names, addresses, phone numbers, and e-mail addresses of family members and relevant friends
- List of traveler's checks, credit cards, and checking account numbers and photocopy of passport & visa (keep separate from the actual items)
- In case of lost luggage, a list of the contents of your luggage (each bag should be labeled inside and out, and the items on your luggage list should be organized according to each bag label) and the contact information for the lost luggage claims for the airline you are using
- Traveler's checks
- Credit cards
- Over-the-counter medications and prescriptions, including eyeglasses
- Insurance policy identity card and a claim form (be sure your health insurance provides for overseas coverage)
- Tour books
- Foreign phrasebook (or electronic translator)
- Eurorail or other passes and tickets obtained in advance of trip
- Miscellaneous travel documents

Packing Tips

🍂 Plan to take as little as possible with you.

🍂 Take essential items, such as cell phones, cameras, travel documents, medicines, toiletries (makeup, shampoo, toothpaste, brush and comb, etc.) and a change of clothing, in your carry-on luggage, in case your checked luggage gets lost.

🍂 Plan a travel wardrobe based around one or two colors and made from wrinkle-resistant polyester, Lycra, or monofiber. Depending on the weather where you are going, a basic wardrobe might include some or all of the following:

- Nightwear
- Underwear
- Shirts/blouses
- Casual pants
- Exercise clothes
- Sweater
- Bathing suit
- Dressy outfit for special evenings
- Raincoat/coat/jacket
- Umbrella
- Hat
- Scarf
- Gloves
- Belts
- Shoes
- Socks/pantyhose
- Jewelry/watch

travel safety tips

• If you become seriously ill or injured abroad, contact a U.S. consular officer. The official can help you locate medical services.

• Record the name, address, and telephone number of someone to be contacted in an emergency. There is a page provided for this information inside your passport.

• If you have a preexisting medical condition, carry a letter from your doctor describing the medical condition and any prescription medications, including the generic name of prescribed drugs.

• Don't take medicine overseas before checking with the foreign embassy to ensure it is not considered an illegal narcotic. If it isn't, store it in its original container and make sure it's labeled clearly.

• Write to the Superintendent of Documents, U.S. Government Printing Office, Washington, DC 20402 and request a list of addresses and telephone numbers of U.S. embassies and consulates abroad.

• For information about diseases, immunizations, and health risks in foreign countries, contact the Government Printing Office to obtain a copy of Health Information for International Travel by the Centers for Disease Control and Prevention (CDC). The CDC maintains the international travelers hotline at 1-877-FYI-TRIP (1-877-394-8747), an automated fax-back service at 1-888-CDC-FAXX (1-888-232-3299) and a home page on the Internet at www.cdc.gov.

• For detailed information on physicians abroad, consult The Official ABMS Directory of Board Certified Medical Specialists published for the American Board of Medical Specialists (available in libraries, U.S. embassies, or from a major credit card company).

For more information on traveling abroad, check out the U.S. Department of State's Web site at www.state.gov.

- Leave a copy of your travel itinerary with family members and friends.
- Request that the post office hold your mail.
- Leave a key to your house with a trusted neighbor or family member,
  or engage a house sitter if you plan to be away for an extended period of time.
- Make sure your homeowner's or renter's insurance is up to date.

A passport is necessary for traveling out of the country (and, after September 11, 2001, it's helpful to have a passport when traveling within the country, as well). Apply several months in advance of your planned departure. If you need visas from foreign embassies, allow more time.

Here is some basic information on obtaining a passport. (*Note*: The following information was accurate to the best of our knowledge at the time of printing, but laws change, and you will have to check with someone in your passport office to confirm the current procedure.)

- You can obtain a passport through a passport agency, by mail-in, at a post office or the office of a clerk of court.
- You can get a passport in an expedited period of time, generally in about two weeks, if you are willing to pay an additional fee and pay for two-way overnight delivery.
- Routine processing takes about six weeks.
- Cash is not accepted for payment. Major credit cards, checks, and money orders are acceptable in most places.
- Forms may be obtained at the post office, through passport agencies, and online at the U.S. Department of State Web site.
- Include your departure date on your application.
- To substantiate your citizenship, you will need a certified copy of your birth certificate (if you don't have one, contact the Vital Statistics office in the state where you were born) and your old, cancelled passport.
- You can apply to renew your passport by mail if you have an undamaged existing passport that was received within the past fif-

teen years and that was issued when you were over the age of sixteen.
- Otherwise, you must apply for your passport in person.
- To obtain a passport, you will need the above-mentioned documentation, a signed form, and two identical passport photographs.
- If your name has changed since an earlier passport was issued, you'll have to enclose a certified copy of the legal document (your marriage certificate) specifying your name change.
- Mail your application in a padded envelope to:

National Passport Center
P. O. Box 371971
Pittsburgh, PA 15250-9971
Write *expedite* on the outside if you are paying for that extra service.
- Include a prepaid overnight return envelope.

Today a bride may choose to retain her own name or take her husband's name. Or, the couple may decide to take hyphenated names, although, for anything other than taking your husband's name or keeping your own, you will probably need to go to court to get an official order changing your name.

To take your husband's name upon marriage, start using it consistently. A certified copy of your marriage certificate, which should be sent to you shortly after your marriage, is required to change your name on important documents such as your Social Security card. Notify government agencies and private institutions of your name change, as well as changing contracts, deeds, and stationery. Here's a partial list of organizations, agencies, and documents affected by a name change.

- Employers
- Post office
- Department of Motor Vehicles
- Department of Records or Vital Statistics
- Banks (checking, savings, brokerage accounts, mortgage payments)
- Voter's registration
- Telephone company
- Tax offices
- Utility companies
- Powers of attorney
- Living wills
- Contracts
- People you owe money to or who owe you money (creditors, loan agencies)
- Insurance companies
- Cable TV company
- Car title
- Business cards
- Medical records and prescriptions
- Club or organization memberships
- Retirement funds
- Alumni or other associations

A wedding may be a romantic celebration, but amidst the joyous preparations, there are a number of business matters that should be attended to. After all, marriage is a legal union that confers both rights and responsibilities on you and your spouse. You need to consider how these will affect your lives and proceed accordingly.

At some point, either right before or shortly after marriage, you will want to consult your tax advisor, insurance expert, and attorney to discuss the ways being married will affect your legal status. Topics you should discuss include:

- Your tax returns
- Financial budgeting and planning
- Insurance policies
- Independent business ownership
- Wills
- Property owned prior to marriage
- Social Security, Medicare, and Disability benefits
- Joint checking accounts
- Trusts
- Government benefits (e.g., veteran's)
- Employment benefits (e.g., health insurance)
- Parenting and custody issues
- Legal benefits and protections provided to spouses under the law
- Premarital agreements to preserve property for children from a previous union

Chapter 9: Four Months Ahead

Arrivals and Departures

Monthly Planner

Sunday	Monday	Tuesday	Wednesday	Thursday	Friday	Saturday

Chapter 9: FOUR MONTHS AHEAD

Arrivals and Departures

Travel is a common component of most weddings. Guests and relatives come in from out of town before the wedding, the bride and groom leave town at the end of the wedding, and in between there's a lot of comings and goings. If you get organized now, and everyone will arrive where they need to be on time and in style.

THIS MONTH'S TO-DO LIST

1. Investigate accommodations for out-of-town guests.

2. Organize transportation.

3. Shop for a going-away outfit.

4. Assemble your trousseau.

5. Look for a place to live.

Guests are responsible for providing their own transportation to and from a wedding. If they live far enough away from the wedding that they need to stay overnight, they are still responsible for making reservations and paying for rooms at a nearby hotel. However, it's a nice gesture when the bride makes planning easier for guests by suggesting suitable and affordable hotels that are close to the wedding location. In many cases, the hotel that has been booked for the reception will offer special discounts for wedding guests. Be sure to ask your catering establishment if such is the case, so you can pass along the information to any out-of-town guests. Even though the wedding is still months off, hotels can fill quickly, especially during popular wedding months, so inform your guests early of their lodging choices.

It's traditional for the groom or his family to pay for lodging for out-of-town groomsmen and for the bride to pay for lodging for any bridesmaids who are coming from a distance. Of course, putting up wedding party members at the home of a nearby friend or relative's house is a perfectly acceptable alternative to paying pricey hotel fees.

Are any of your out-of-town guests unfamiliar with the area where your wedding is being held? Share what you know about the area, so they have the option of making a fun and relaxing mini-vacation out of the trip. Put together a "welcome packet." You might contact your local chamber of commerce for informational brochures about exciting things to do and see in the town and surrounding area, maps, and car rental agencies. Because your guests will want to look their best, you can include information about beauty salons, spas, and drycleaning services. You'll save your guests time and trouble and free them up to enjoy partying with you!

Out-of-Town Guest Welcome Packet

- Hotels and inns
- Sights to see
- Rental cars
- Maps
- Travel guide (check with your local automobile club, if you are a member)
- Local newspaper or magazine
- Golf courses
- Spas and beauty salons
- Local events
- Shopping destinations
- Drycleaners and laundry services
- Restaurants
- Drugstores

GIFT BASKETS

Another way to make life easier for out-of-town guests is to create gift baskets filled with useful sundries, such as gourmet coffee packets, needles, thread and pins, pantyhose, and other small but useful necessities that people need in emergencies. Enclose a note with your basket or welcome packet saying how much you appreciate the guest(s) coming such a long way to celebrate your special day with you.

TRANSPORTATION

There are many romantic ways to arrive at and depart from your wedding. Here are some ideas:

Coaches & Carriages

These include antique coaches, Victorian carriages, surreys, horse-drawn trolleys, sleighs, and carts. Drivers often dress in vintage attire. Transportation area is limited to the number of miles a horse can pull a carriage in the allotted time. Often, mileage to and from the site is included in the total.

Hot-air Balloons

Some balloons hold as many as seven people (including the pilot). Many serve complimentary sparkling wine to the couple after the flight. This is a whimsical way to leave. Flights typically are an hour long and some pilots are ordained ministers and can conduct the wedding ceremony itself. Tethered balloons make a fun entertainment at a reception.

Vintage Cars

Travel in style in a vintage car with a chauffeur in a tuxedo. The average limo service will travel up to two or three hours away.

Limousines

Most limousines are rented by the hour, day, or half-day. The cost usually includes the driver, although most expect a gratuity on top of the advertised rate. Make sure the fee includes the gas. Rates are determined by size and model/make. Fancy and vintage limousines are booked early and cost the most money.

THE BRIDE'S TROUSSEAU

"Trousseau" is a French word meaning "little bundle." Since the nineteenth century, it has been used to refer to the goods the bride brought with her into her marriage. Traditionally, the trousseau consisted of articles of clothing as well as household furnishings and equipment, including pots and pans, bed linens, and tableware. With her trousseau, the bride could set up house overnight.

In the olden days, many girls started assembling their trousseau at an early age. A "hope chest" would be given to the girl by her parents, and she would spend her young years sewing things to put in it in preparation for a future marriage. Quilts, tablecloths,

bed linens, and nightgowns made up a good portion of the hope chest's contents.

As times changed, more goods became manufactured, and the bridal registry came into being, the word "trousseau" became a reference to the bride's clothing, especially her going-away outfit and negligee.

Today, the trousseau has become more associated with lingerie than anything else.

Lingerie Dos

- Go to a specialty store and get correct measurements.
- Consider a longline strapless bra for the greatest amount of support.
- Try lingerie on with your gown so you choose a support garment that works with the cut and shape of your dress.
- If your bridal gown has a full skirt, buy a crinoline slip or hoops to wear under it. They come in varying widths; make sure your slip has the correct fullness to lift your skirt without being too full.
- Set a blue ribbon in the waistband of your crinoline or at the waist inside the bridal gown itself — it's a bridal "good luck" tradition.

- If you wish to wear a garter, there are many handmade ones that will make beautiful keepsakes. Or, you can make one yourself with a bit of elastic, ribbon, lace, and charms that are personally symbolic.
- Select a peignoir set that makes the most of your coloring and enhances your body type.

One of the most helpful tasks you can do in preparation for your wedding day and future married life is clean out your closet. Whether you are moving into an apartment or a house with your intended, storage space is likely to be at a premium. You may even find yourself sharing a closet with your husband. Moving itself is a tough job. Anything you can do to cut down on the number of items being moved is a good idea.

Sorting your Clothes

1. Make an initial pass on the items in your wardrobe. Set aside any item that does not pass these criteria:
• Fit (i.e., it fits or is worth altering)
• Comfort
• Usefulness
• Versatility (you can wear it with several other articles of clothing)
• Color
• Style
• You've worn it in the past year
• Little or no signs of wear and tear

2. Take the clothes that do not pass the above criteria and donate them to a thrift shop.

3. Divide the remaining items by season: winter, summer, and transitional (meaning it can be worn in most seasons).

4. If you don't have a lot of time, concentrate on the upcoming season. Put the clothes for other times of the year in storage boxes or containers until you have time to deal with them. Be sure to label the exterior of the containers so you know what is in them. If possible, put clothes in the containers according to season or purpose.

5. Try the remaining clothes on in front of a mirror to be sure the really do pass the criteria.

6. Clean, press, make alterations, and mend items that you plan to keep.

7. Arrange the items in an appropriate storage unit. As you hang them in the closet or fold them flat in a drawer, keep similar items together.

8. Make a list of new clothing items that you need to purchase. (Keep in mind the above criteria!) In addition to buying replacements for items you just discarded, consider whether you are moving or traveling to another part of the country, starting a new job, or need a few things for wedding-related functions, such as a going-away outfit. A traditional going-away outfit was a feminine-style suit or dress with gloves and a hat, but more than one contemporary bride has exited in leather on a Harley Davidson. It all depends on your style.

9. Figure out what hardware and storage units you will need to create a neatly organized closet in your new place. (It's not too late to add some closet organizers to your registry list, if they aren't on it already.)

CLOTHING STORAGE TIPS

• Hang items on separate hangers

• Choose hangers appropriate for the clothing item (e.g., pants on pants hangers, etc.)

• Use cloth fabric bags instead of plastic ones; chemicals in plastic can leach out and discolor fabric.

• Keep acid-free tissue paper on hand and layer it between clothing when separating garments.

• Roll knit and casual clothing around tissue and place in drawers to keep it wrinkle-free.

SHOPPING FOR LUGGAGE

The hope chest may be a thing of the past, but luggage is not. Choose waterproof luggage with reinforced handles and double stitching. Here are some standard pieces you should consider purchasing in a waterproof material.

• Carry-on bag (14 x 22 inches, but this may be subject to change, be sure to check with the airlines) of soft- or hard-sided construction, small enough to fit under an airplane seat or in an overhead compartment for lingerie, change of clothing, and sundries.

• Pullman (28- x 30-inches), for jackets, skirts, and blouses. For convenience, look for one that has wheels.

• Hanging garment bag with pockets for shoes or accessories and a shoulder strap.

If you haven't already, you soon will start to receive wedding gifts. Thank-you notes should be sent as soon as possible after the gift arrives, and no later than eight weeks after its receipt. Since the next few months will be busy, take time now to stock up on some beautiful cards or fine stationery in a neutral color, pens, and stamps so you have them at your disposal whenever you need to write a thank-you. If you are short on time, you can send a card custom-printed with a special thank-you message, but don't forget to follow up with a personal note at some point. Write from the heart, and mention the specific gift, and tell the reader how much you will enjoy using it. By the way, it is perfectly acceptable for the groom to write thank-yous — in fact, this is one task both of you should do together!

Buying a House

Owning your own home is a newlywed's dream. If you plan to buy a house within the first year of marriage, start shopping now. Get familiar with the real estate market in the area where you plan to live. Get the best rate you can. Find an advisor who can explain the difference between a fixed, balloon, and adjustable rate mortgage and who can do the math for you. Familiarize yourself with hidden lender's fees, loan origination fees, points, closing costs, and other costs related to processing applications. Familiarize yourself with construction techniques, building materials, and how to identify age-related wear that can cost a lot of money to repair versus minor repairs that are cosmetic facelifts. A house is one of the biggest investments you can make. Plan your purchase carefully.

Chapter 10: THREE MONTHS AHEAD

Symbols of Commitment

Monthly Planner

Sunday	Monday	Tuesday	Wednesday	Thursday	Friday	Saturday

Chapter 10: THREE MONTHS AHEAD

Symbols of Commitment

Despite all your preparation, until now, the actual wedding might still have seemed like a distant dream. But now you are choosing a circle of gold or silver that will symbolize your love from the day your intended slips the ring on your finger. And you are finally going to mail out invitations, imprinted with the actual date.

THIS MONTH'S TO-DO LIST

1. Choose a wedding ring.

2. Select bridal jewelry.

3. Mail your invitations.

4. Learn to dance.

In the past, men did not always wear wedding bands. Times have changed. Today most couples treasure the trip to the jewelry store to choose their wedding bands together. Rings are the only wedding purchases that the bride and groom will enjoy every day for years to come. As symbols of commitment, fidelity, and honor, rings are tokens most couples take the time to choose carefully.

In the traditional Western wedding, the engagement ring and the wedding band are both worn on the left ring finger, which in folklore is said to run straight to the heart.

When shopping for rings, work with a reputable jeweler. Ask for an appraisal certificate so you can insure your rings for the value of their replacement.

Gold is the traditional metal, but platinum is surging in popularity. One of the rarest of all precious metals, and therefore somewhat expensive, platinum is also a hard metal that resists scratches and can last up to fifty years without showing signs of wear. Platinum jewelry also does not require any special care, but

can be electro- or rhodium-plated with another precious metal, to help preserve its luster. Compared with gold, which is 58 percent pure for 14 karat, for platinum there is a 90% pure standard, which is why many feel that, although platinum costs more, it is a better investment. Still others prefer yellow gold for its coloring.

Today, you can find a number of cutting-edge ring designs, with unique surface treatments, bold, sculptural lines, and fancy colored stone accents, as well as reproductions of antique designs from original dies in both masculine and feminine styles. There are also many craftsmen who will gladly custom-design your rings upon request.

Wedding Ring Worksheet

Jewelry Store Name:		Phone No.:	
Address:		E-mail:	
		Web site:	

ITEM:	DESCRIPTION:	COST:	IN STOCK/ORDER :	COMMENTS:

Jewelry Store Name:		Phone No.:	
Address:		E-mail:	
		Web site:	

ITEM:	DESCRIPTION:	COST:	IN STOCK/ORDER :	COMMENTS:

Jewelry Store Name:		Phone No.:	
Address:		E-mail:	
		Web site:	

ITEM:	DESCRIPTION:	COST:	IN STOCK/ORDER :	COMMENTS:

Pearls

The wedding ring is not the only piece of jewelry that is traditionally present at weddings. A pearl necklace and earrings have been a bridal custom since medieval times, and possibly earlier.

Jewelry was a popular gift for aristocratic medieval brides, who wore hair ornaments, coronals, and hairbands decorated with pearls and other gems. By the late fifteenth century, crowns and coronals were replaced with elaborate headdresses, called "crowns of marriage." Beginning in the Middle Ages, poor brides could rent marriage crowns and parures (or ensemble of matching necklace, earrings, hair comb, pin, and bracelet) from the local church or town hall to wear on her wedding day. This custom of renting bridal jewelry from the town survived well into the nineteenth century in Europe. Seed-pearl embroidery on wedding gowns has become a bridal tradition, although today the pearls tend to be made of glass, resin, or even plastic.

The custom of giving pearls to brides, and of brides wearing pearl necklaces and earrings on their wedding day, has continued through modern times. In the 1950s, Prince Rainier of Monaco pledged his love to Grace Kelly with a necklace and earrings of pearls and diamonds. Diana, Princess of Wales, received a pearl tiara as a wedding present.

Today, natural pearls are all but extinct because of water pollution. The only natural pearls available to modern brides are sold at estate jewelry sales. In 1920, Japanese Kokichi Mikimoto created a patented process that enabled the production of great numbers of round, lustrous pearls that involves inserting a mother-of-pearl bead (made from the shell of a freshwater American mollusk) and a piece of mantle from one oyster, into another oyster. Mikimoto also developed a grading system for pearls, which today is the industry standard.

To calculate the price of pearl, first the pearl is weighed. The weight in grains is then multiplied by the base price, which depends on the shape, color, the luster, and surface appearance of the pearl. Poor quality pearls are assigned a C rating, followed by B, A, AA, AAA, Fine, and Gem. Some companies have instituted in-between grades, such as A+. Most of the pearls sold in the United States are graded A+ or AA.

tips for pearl maintenance

Each time you wear cultured pearls, wipe them down with a fine cloth to get rid of any perfume, cosmetics, or dirt. Store them in a jewelry box or flannel bag. Take them to your jeweler to be restrung and cleaned at least once a year.

Colored Gemstones

Color is the principal determinant of value in colored gemstones. Light, the type of light and its intensity, or brightness, affects it. As a general rule, the closer a colored gemstone comes to being the pure spectral hue of that color, the better the color. Many brides prefer colored gemstones to the traditional diamonds and pearls for sentimental reasons, such as an attachment to a color or a particular stone's legendary properties.

Although more than 2,000 natural minerals are known to exist, fewer than 100 are used as gemstones, and only certain gemstones, such as rubies, emeralds, and sapphires, have gained importance.

Perhaps that is why royal grooms often give their brides colored gemstones. Take, for instance, the Prince Albert Brooch, a wedding gift given to Queen Victoria by Prince Albert on February 9, 1840. This pledge of undying love consisted of a large sapphire, surrounded by twelve round diamonds.

Another favorite of royal brides is the bridal crown set with colored gemstones. One such famous crown appeared in Germany in 1402. King Henry IV of England gave it to his daughter, Princess Blanche, as part of their dowry on her marriage to the Elector Palatine, Ludwig III of Bavaria. This crown, kept in the Residenz Museum in Munich, is elaborately decorated with aquamarines, pearls, sapphires, rubies, and emeralds.

Green emeralds, from the beryl family, are said to break at the moment of marital infidelity. They are considered to be more valuable than fancy colored diamonds, and second only to rubies. Today, many women are happy to receive emeralds. This fascination dates back to the days of Queen Cleopatra's vast emerald mines, located by the Egyptian Red Sea.

Contemporary brides often choose an alternative three-stone engagement ring over the diamond solitaire to be worn both as engagement ring and wedding band.

With today's technology, it is possible to enhance colored gemstones in a variety of ways. Still, one of the most commonly encountered and commercially accepted methods of enhancement is heat enhancement. The process may lighten, darken, or completely change the color of the gemstone. The color obtained is usually permanent and is performed on rubies, sapphires, and the like.

Radiation, a controversial method of enhancement, sometimes used in conjunction with heat enhancement, usually gives a permanent color change. Both methods are used on sapphires and fancy colored diamonds.

A new treatment to enhance fancy colored diamonds is called fracture filling. It is used for low-clarity gemstones. The process involves filling the inclusions with glass under pressure.

Oiling, an extremely rare technique used on emeralds, involves filling fine cracks of the gemstone with oil to improve color. In general, the more cracks on an emerald, the more white space visible. Again, this is also a controversial practice because green oils, considered unethical by jewelers, mask the natural inclusions of the colored gemstone.

Waxing, a color enhancement process is used on star rubies and sapphires, involves the rubbing of a gemstone with a tinted waxlike substance to hide surface cracks and blemishes and slightly improve color.

Colored gemstones can also be stained or dyed. Dyeing is used to intensify the color of pale gemstones, as well as to give color to almost colorless stones.

Along with instruments, jewelers use a variety of systems to grade colored gemstones. Unlike pearls, there is no universal grading system. Since gemstones are different from each other, there is no easy way to devise a universal system. For example, the Gemological Institute of America must use a machine that measures color, called the Color Master, along with a set of over 300 plastic colored gemstones that must be compared with the real colored gemstones.

The color grading for colored gemstones is not as exact as the system for fancy colored diamonds. For instance, the Gemological Institute of America uses a letter system. D is the top of the line, E, F, G, H, and I are colorless to the naked eye, J, K, and L appear colorless, and M through Z include gemstones that become increasingly yellowish to downright dim.

Flaw classification is a criterion in determining the value of colored gemstones. The Gemological Institute of America's grading system is the main method used in the United States. This system indicates a greater number of classifications, thereby providing greater precision in determining the flaw grade. The system utilizes nine grades, FL (no visible flaws, internal or external), VVS1 and VVS2 (very, very slightly imperfect), VS1 and VS2 (very slightly imperfect), SI1 and SI2 (slightly imperfect), and I1 and I2 (imperfect or included). You can see some of these flaws with the naked eye, but gemstones of all grades are sold because people are more willing to accept imperfections because of a lower price.

Finally, get a certification of origin for the gemstone, especially if it has a geographical name attached to it. This authentication is important because gemstones have been sold in the past as if they were more valuable and of a higher grade than they actually were. Two labs specializing in these certificates include the American Geological Laboratory and the Gubelin Laboratory.

• Mail wedding invitations no later than four to six weeks prior to the wedding.

• The traditional wedding invitation is placed with any additional cards (such as the reception and rsvp cards) inside in an ungummed envelope. The ungummed envelope is then slipped into an outer envelope that is gummed. A piece of tissue paper protects the printed face of the invitation from smudging.

• Many brides today hire calligraphers to address their envelopes. The full name of the guest, including any appropriate titles, such as *Dr.* or *Mrs.*

• Put the return address on the front of the envelope.

• Include a map to the reception and ceremony locations as a courtesy to your guests.

• Take a sample to the post office to weigh before buying and applying the stamps. Many invitations require extra postage.

One of the most breathtaking — and sentimental moments — at a wedding reception is the couple's first dance. A close second is the bride's dance with her dad.

Unfortunately, many couples today simply do not know how to ballroom dance. To make a beautiful impression on the dance floor, now is the time to sign up for some lessons.

The waltz is an easy dance to begin with. Its basic box step provides a nice foundation for many other dance steps.

A dance teacher can choreograph a special dance for the two of you. Practicing the dance routine frequently will help you get the steps down. As you become more comfortable on your feet, you will feel more at ease improvising steps to different kinds of music.

As an aside, ballroom dance shoes, with their suede soles and steel shanks, make excellent bridal shoes.

DANCE WORKSHEET

SCHOOL	NAME	ADDRESS	COST	TIMES/DANCES TAUGHT

Chapter 11: Two Months Ahead

Finishing Touches

Monthly Planner

Sunday	Monday	Tuesday	Wednesday	Thursday	Friday	Saturday

Chapter 11: Two Months Ahead

Finishing Touches

Now is the time to attend to all the odds and ends that you have put off while making the much bigger, flashier wedding decisions. But let there be no mistake: there won't be a wedding without following through on these essential details, so get busy!

THIS MONTH'S TO-DO LIST

1. Finalize the ceremony.

2. Plan the rehearsal dinner.

3. Obtain blood tests.

4. Get a marriage license.

This is the time to slow down and take a look at what you've accomplished and what tasks still lie ahead. The program book can be one of the most enduring memories of your wedding ceremony. It's also a good tool to help finalize aspects of your special day. The rehearsal dinner presents an opportunity to iron out any glitches as you run through the ceremony. It can also be an occasion that allows a relaxed setting where disparate guests and family members have time to get to know each other. The nitty gritty chores of the blood tests and marriage certificate will soon be under your belt.

With the technological advances that have happened in the printing industry in the past few years, printing up programs books and pew cards is no longer as difficult and time-consuming as it used to be. But with so much still to be done for the wedding, it is wise to get as much of the printing done in advance as possible.

Your program book will serve as a memento for your special day. A nice touch is to print the cover on a beautiful decorative paper, and then to tie a ribbon, elastic thread, or cording around the middle of the booklet to give it a special flourish. By now you should have a clear idea of:

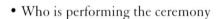

- Who is performing the ceremony
- Where it will be held
- Who you wedding party members are
- Which musicians will be playing at your ceremony
- The structure of the ceremony
- Highlights of the ceremony, such as a song or a poem that is read

These are the items to include in your ceremony book, along with any special remembrances, messages, or thank-yous.

Program Book Planner

Program books are printed and bound in signatures of four pages each, so your book will always have an even number of pages. Knowing this can help you plan the contents. List the contents of each page of your program book on the lines to the left of the square boxes, below. Use the boxes to sketch graphic ideas or play with color.

Length of book:

Front cover:

Contents:

Page 1 Contents:

Page 2 Contents:

Page 3 Contents:

Page 4 Contents:

Page 5 Contents:

Page 6 Contents:

Page 7 Contents:

Page 8 Contents:

Back cover contents:

Rehearsal time:

Date:

Location:

Items I need to bring with me (e.g., "fake" bouquet, readings, ring-bearer pillow):

Who should attend:

Your wedding is too important to be left to chance. Typically on the night preceding the wedding, the bridal party and close family members will attend a scheduled rehearsal at the place of worship or other ceremony location.

Often, more than one couple will be rehearsing on the same evening, so it's important to arrive on time.

After a quick walk-through, it's time to kick back a little and relax with family, friends, and the groom, of course! This is likely to be the last time you see each other before the big day.

A private room in a restaurant or banquet hall is usually the best place for the rehearsal dinner, although, if money is an issue, a family member can host it at home. Traditionally, the groom's family hosted the rehearsal dinner. However, today it is not unusual for the bride's family or even the couple themselves to host this party.

The guest list includes all members of the wedding party, the officiant and his or her spouse, and any close friends or family members who attended the rehearsal.

This is often the appropriate time for the bride and groom to give their wedding party members gifts to thank them for their help throughout the past months and to pay the officiant's fee. It is also the time when the wedding party toasts the bride and groom spontaneously and without reservations.

Rehearsal Dinner

Rehearsal time:

Date:

Location:

Who should attend:

A marriage license is a legal document that authorizes you to get married. Apply for your marriage license at the county clerk's office in the county or town in the state where you want to be married. The fee for the license is nominal. There is often a wait of a few days before you will receive the license. Some states also require an additional waiting period before you can get married. A marriage license is good for thirty days to a year, depending on the state.

The minimum age for marriage without parental consent is eighteen in all fifty states. You should apply in person at the courthouse in the county in which you are getting married, unless otherwise directed by a town official. Certified copies are required for official documents. There are some different requirements for obtaining a license among the states.

For example, in some states both parties must appear in person at the courthouse to apply. No witnesses are necessary. Blood test results from your physician taken within the last twenty-five days are required. A driver's license can be used to provide proof of age. There is an application fee, and the waiting period before the license can be received is seventy-two hours. Once issued, the license remains valid for thirty days to a year, depending on the state. Anyone may pick up the license. For second marriages, a divorce decree (at least thirty days old) or proof of death is required.

In another state, if the bride is a resident, the license is applied for in her municipality's Registrar of Vital Statistics. If she is not a resident, but the groom is, the license should be issued by his municipality's Registrar. Under these two circumstances, the license can be used anywhere in the state. The bride and groom do not have to apply together, but both parties must complete the application before the license is issued with the same witness. They must present signed and dated blood test results from their physician no more than thirty days old. The application fee is $8 in cash. Proof of age, such as a driver's license, is required. There is a seventy-two hour waiting period. Once issued, the license is valid for thirty days. For second marriages, copies of divorce papers or death certificates must be shown.

In other states, both parties are required to apply in person at the county courthouse. No witnesses are required. No blood test is required, and a waiting period is mandatory before the license can be received. Once applied for, the license may be picked up anytime within the next three months. For those under twenty-one, proof of age must be provided with a birth certificate, and those over twenty-one can show a driver's license. Information about any previous marriages must be given under oath before the Deputy Clerk of Court at the time of application.

The bottom line is, call your local county courthouse or municipal office well in advance of your wedding date for more information. If you are planning a civil service, call to find out who is available to perform the ceremony and the fees involved. The person who performs the ceremony is responsible for filing the license, blood test results and marriage certificate after the wedding with the Registrar (or other appropriate official) of the county in which the ceremony took place. Be sure to follow up and verify that this has been done to avoid any problems in the future.

THE MARRIAGE CERTIFICATE

Just after your wedding ceremony, you, your spouse, the person who officiated, and one or two witnesses, will sign the marriage certificate.

Within a few days of your wedding, the person who married you (clergy, justice of the peace, or judge) will file the marriage certificate with the appropriate county official (depending on the state, this may be the registrar, clerk, or recorder). You will then be sent a certified copy of this certificate two weeks or so after you're married. The certified document you receive is your official proof of marriage.

Check with the county clerk's office in the town you plan to marry for the up-to-date policy on marriage certificates.

BLOOD TESTS

Blood tests for couples planning to marry are no longer required by most states, but some do still require them. The purpose of these tests was to screen for a sexually transmitted disease (STD), rubella (measles), and genetic disorders such as sickle-cell anemia or Tay-Sachs disease.

Some states may refuse to issue a marriage license if either individual tests positive for a venereal disease. Check with the county clerk's office in the town you plan to marry for the up-to-date policy on blood tests.

who can officiate at a wedding?

A justice of the peace, judge, or court clerk who has legal authority to perform marriages officiates at civil weddings. A clergy member (priest, minister, or rabbi) conducts religious ceremonies. Tribal chiefs officiate at Native American weddings, although a tribe may sometimes grant another person the authority to officiate at weddings.

PARENTS' DAYS

As a thank-you for all your parents have done and are doing for you, invite each of them to spend time with you as their special day. Invite Mom to lunch after shopping for *her* gown or spend a few hours with Dad on the golf course. Opportunities to spend one-on-one time with your parents will become fewer and farther between as you get caught up in your own adult life and perhaps even have children. Give your mom and dad the gift of some quality time now. It will mean the world to them.

choosing a gift for the groom or bride

The custom of brides and grooms exchanging gifts with one another in commemoration of their wedding is a lovely wedding tradition. The gift should be long-lasting and have sentimental value for the receiver. It does not have to be expensive.

Chapter 12: ONE MONTH AHEAD

Countdown to Bliss

This is the month when all of your hard work over the past year bears fruit. It's one of the busiest months in the wedding-planning process, but by now, you should have things pretty much under control. Yes, your excitement — and the excitement of those around you — is mounting; yes, there are butterflies in your stomach; yes, there are tons of small items to check up on, but as long as you follow this month's "To-Dos" and checklists, and you won't overlook a thing!

THIS MONTH'S TO-DO LIST
FOUR WEEKS IN ADVANCE:

1. Pick up your gown and make final alterations.
2. Confirm dates and details with service personnel.
3. Contact newspaper.
4. Choose gifts for participants.
5. Finalize your guest list.
6. Make seating arrangements and obtain placecards.
7. Create a wedding day timetable, and distribute task cards to wedding party.
8. Your rehearsal dinner.
9. Wedding day itinerary.

or the next four weeks, your life will be one long to-do list, so we've organized this final chapter to reflect this reality. But rest assured, if you followed the steps we've outlined so far, you'll already have most of the items on the following lists started. Now it's just a matter of finalizing all of the projects you've got going.

Congratulations — you've made it this far!

1. Coordinate final arrangements for the groom's attire and that of his groomsmen.

2. Review your honeymoon plans, and organize packing, tickets, travel documents, and currency.

3. Have a final fitting for the wedding gown. Don't forget to bring undergarments and shoes.

4. Make sure the attendants have picked up their outfits and that the dresses fit. Arrange for alterations if necessary.

5. Book a restaurant for the rehearsal dinner, and issue invitations.

6. Arrange the bachelor and bachelorette parties.

7. Visit your hairstylist with your headpiece to plan the final look for your wedding day.

Two weeks in advance:

1. Pick up your gown.

2. Contact the caterer to finalize guest numbers, menu, and seating arrangements.

3. Compile your final guest list.

4. Get your marriage license.

5. Confirm out-of-town-guest lodging.

6. Confirm the duties, time, and function of all booked services. In addition to the caterer, these include, but are not limited to, the band, transportation, clergy, church, photographer, videographer. (See the categories listed on planning sheets in Chapter 1.)

7. Visit the post office to arrange for mail to be held while you're away and, if necessary, to file change-of-address forms.

One week in advance:

1. Prepare a travel itinerary, and deliver it to appropriate people.

2. Prepare final wedding itinerary for wedding-party members.

3. Write place cards, or pick them up from the calligrapher.

4. Write checks for final balances.

5. Write checks and put them in separate envelopes for the offciant, organist, and choir.

6. Shop for sundries (sunscreen, film, for example).

7. Contact the newspaper about your wedding announcement.

8. Call the bakery, and confirm cake delivery to reception hall.

9. Reconfirm flight plans and tickets.

The day before:

1. Pick up the rental tuxedos.

2. Pick up the rental cars.

3. Greet out-of-town guests.

4. Assemble the bride's emergency kit (needle and thread, safety pins, aspirin, pantyhose, tissues, and so forth).

5. Attend your wedding rehearsal.

6. Review seating instructions and pew cards with the ushers.

7. Distribute task cards (see the section in the back of the book).

8. Attend the rehearsal dinner.

9. Give the wedding party their gifts.

10. Give the best men the money in envelopes to deliver to the officiant, etc.

On the day of the wedding:

1. Eat breakfast.

2. Have your hair styled and get a professional makeup application.

3. Accept delivery of flowers.

4. Welcome bridesmaids at home or in dressing room.

5. Get dressed.

6. Pose for preceremony photographs.

7. Get into a car and drive to ceremony site.

8. Take part in ceremony.

9. Pose for postceremony photographs.

10. Arrive at reception where cocktail party is in progress.

11. Make an entrance!

12. Dance your first dance as a couple.

13. If you wish, groom will remove your garter.

14. Initiate cutting the cake.

15. Throw your bouquet.

16. Leave for the after-party or honeymoon.

Afterward:

1. Attend the after-reception party or brunch.

2. Deposit gifts of money.

3. Get changed and leave for your honeymoon.

4. Have your gown preserved.

5. Write thank-you notes.

6. Pick up your wedding photos and video.

7. Mail the photos to your wedding party, relatives, and friends.

8. Change your name if you wish.

Note: With the exception of the head tables, which tend to be rectangular, most tables sit six, eight, or ten people for dinner. (Cocktail tables tend to be much smaller, seating two to four people. But you do not need a seating plan for cocktails.) Ask your banquet hall director how many tables are planned and how many people can be seated at each table. Male and female guests usually alternate seating.

GUEST #	TABLE #	SEAT #	GUEST NAME
1			
2			
3			
4			
5			
6			
7			
8			
9			
10			
11			
12			
13			
14			
15			
16			
17			
18			
19			
20			
21			
22			
23			
24			
25			
26			
27			

Reception Seating Chart

GUEST #	TABLE #	SEAT #	GUEST NAME
28			
29			
30			
31			
32			
33			
34			
35			
36			
37			
38			
39			
40			
41			
42			
43			
44			
45			
46			
47			
48			
49			
50			
51			
52			
53			
54			
55			
56			
57			
58			
59			

Reception Seating Chart

GUEST #	TABLE #	SEAT #	GUEST NAME
60			
61			
62			
63			
64			
65			
66			
67			
68			
69			
70			
71			
72			
73			
74			
75			
76			
77			
78			
79			
80			
81			
82			
83			
84			
85			
86			
87			
88			
89			
90			
91			

GUEST #	TABLE #	SEAT #	GUEST NAME
92			
93			
94			
95			
96			
97			
98			
99			
100			
101			
102			
103			
104			
105			
106			
107			
108			
109			
110			
111			
112			
113			
114			
115			
116			
117			
118			
119			
120			
121			
122			
123			

RECEPTION SEATING CHART

GUEST #	TABLE #	SEAT #	GUEST NAME
124			
125			
126			
127			
128			
129			
130			
131			
132			
133			
134			
135			
136			
137			
138			
139			
140			
141			
142			
143			
144			
145			
146			
147			
148			
149			
150			
151			
152			
153			
154			
155			

RECEPTION SEATING CHART

GUEST #	TABLE #	SEAT #	GUEST NAME
156			
157			
158			
159			
160			
161			
162			
163			
164			
165			
166			
167			
168			
169			
170			
171			
172			
173			
174			
175			
176			
177			
178			
179			
180			
181			
182			
183			
184			
185			
186			
187			

You will depend on the help of many service people to create the wedding of your dreams. Gratuities are usually included in reception hall fees for the banquet waitstaff. However, you will probably have occasion to tip many other service people during the wedding day and the honeymoon that follows. Here's a basic guide to tipping fees. Naturally, if someone goes the extra mile, feel free to tip more.

- Bellhops, porters at airports and train stations: $1 per bag. Bellhops get tipped twice: when they show you to your room and when you leave it.
- Bus drivers on group tours: $1 for four hours
- Chambermaid: $1-2 per day
- Cloakroom attendant: $1-2
- Concierge at hotel: $2 and up for filling special request, such as booking a theater reservation
- Doormen: $1 to hail a taxi, whether by phone or on the street
- Ladies room attendant: .25-.50 cents
- Maid: $1 per night
- Parking garage attendant: $1-2
- Taxi and limo drivers: 15% of the fare
- Tour guides for group tours: $1 for four hours
- Valet parking: $1 to park or retrieve your car
- Waiters (including room service): 15 to 20% of your pretax check

man's best friend

The best man plays a special role in the wedding celebration. Traditionally, it's his responsibility to keep the groom on track with numerous responsibilities.

It's the best man who helps the groom manage details of the tuxedo rental and honeymoon planning. He arranges the bachelor party. He holds the checks that are delivered to ceremony participants the day of the wedding. He organizes the ushers. The best man is the keeper of the wedding bands. He reads messages from well-wishers who could not attend, toasts the couple, and collects the groom to deliver him to the ceremony site.

- If you want to preserve your gown for years down the road as an heirloom, consult someone familiar with textile preservation at a local museum to find out which cleaner will best preserve your gown.
- Fold the gown in acid-free tissue paper.
- Wrap it in unbleached muslin
- Lay it flat or folded in a dark, dry place, preferably a cedar-lined chest or drawer.
- Take it out once a year to air it.
- Avoid having plastic materials contact your dress. They will yellow it.

The organizations listed below have mission statements whose goal is to provide some kind of resource to people who are getting married. They have been around for many years and have member locator services or listings, so we are including them as a possible help to readers. The information was current at the time of printing. Inclusion in this book does not constitute an endorsement on the part of its authors. As is the case with any service, we recommend that you practice common sense and due diligence when contacting the members of any organization, including the ones on the list below.

Professional Photographers of America, Inc.
229 Peachtree St. NE, Suite 2200
Atlanta, GA 30303
PPA Service Center
(800) 786-6277
or (404) 522-8600
Fax: (404) 614-6400
www.ppa.com

According to its Web site, PPA is the world's leading certifying agency for imaging professionals and the world's largest not-for-profit association for professional photographers. PPA offers consumers free referrals to photographic professionals, as well as acting as a locator service for finding the owners of images.

Wedding and Portrait Photographers International
P.O. Box 2003
1312 Lincoln Boulevard
Santa Monica, CA USA 90406-2003
(310) 451-0090
Fax: (310) 395-9058
www.wppinow.com/eventphoto/
Another well-known association of wedding photographers.

American Society of Travel Agents
1101 King Street, Ste. 200
Alexandria, VA 22314
(703) 739-2782
Fax: (703) 684-8319
www.astanet.com/about/index.asp

ASTA, according to its Web site, is the world's largest association of travel professionals, with 20,000-plus members including travel agents and the companies whose products they sell such as tours, cruises, hotels, car rentals, etc.

The Wedding and Event Videographers Association International

8499 S. Tamiami Trail, PMB 208
Sarasota, FL 34238
(941) 923-5334
Fax: (941) 921-3836
www.weva.com
According to its Web site, WEVA is the largest nonprofit trade association representing professional wedding and event videographers.

U.S. Department of State

http://travel.state.gov/
www.state.gov/travel/
This Web site contains information issued by the U.S. State department regarding travel abroad. For official forms, including passport forms, see:
www.state.gov/m/a/dir/c4455.htm

The American Disc Jockey Association

2000 Corporate Drive #408
Ladera Ranch, CA 92694
(888) 723-5776
The ADJA is an association of professional mobile entertainers.

Association of Wedding Gown Specialists

www.weddinggownspecialists.com
According to the AWGS Web site, it has Wedding Gown Specialists® represented in more than 500 cities around the world who specialize in caring for wedding gowns, both old and new. It features trademarked MuseumCare™ preservations.

Association of Bridal Consultants

200 Chestnutland Rd.
New Milford, CT 06776-2521
(860) 355-0464
Fax: (860) 354-1404
E-mail: office@bridalassn.com
The Association of Bridal Consultants is a professional organization for the wedding industry. In existence since 1981, according to its Web site it has almost 2,900 members in 19 countries on six continents.

NOTES

Maid of Honor

Arrival time: _____

Location: _____

Other: _____

At the Ceremony

- Prior to ceremony, help the bride get dressed
- Precede the bride, as well as flower girl and ring bearer, down the aisle
- Arrange bride's train and veil after the bride walks down the aisle and before actual ceremony
- Hold groom's wedding band during the ceremony
- During vows and exchange of rings, hold the bride's bouquet
- Straighten bride's train and, with best man, follows couple down the aisle after ceremony
- Sign marriage certificate as a witness

At the Reception

- Accompany bride and groom for pictures
- Arrange bride's bustle and veil prior to reception entrance
- Stand in the receiving line
- Sit at the head table to the groom's left
- Toast the couple
- Dance with best man during the formal dance introducing wedding party

Afterwards

- Help bride change for honeymoon
- Help keep track of gifts

Best Man

Arrival time: _____

Location: _____

Other: _____

At the Ceremony

- Coordinates transportation
- Organize ushers
- Act as groom's valet
- Stand next to groom during ceremony
- Hold bride's wedding band during the ceremony
- Together with maid of honor, exit down the aisle after the ceremony
- Hold clergy and ceremony fees and cash for tipping
- Sign marriage certificate as a witness

At the Reception

- Accompany bride and groom for pictures
- Traditionally, you do not stand in the receiving line (although this custom is changing)
- Sit at the head table to the bride's right
- Gives first toast to the bride
- During the first dance, dance with maid of honor

Afterwards

- Organizes keys, luggage, and getaway
- After the wedding, return groom's tuxedo or other rentals

Groomsman (photocopy if more than one)

Arrival time: _____

Location: _____

Other: _____

At the Ceremony

- Assist with last-minute preparations
- Review seating areas for special guests
- Seat guests appropriately upon arrival (bride's guests to the left, groom's guests to the right)
- Offer arm when seating single female guests
- Seat bride's mother in first pew on left and seat groom's mother in first pew on right
- Lay aisle runner and loop ribbons over pews
- Proceed up the aisle in pairs prior to processional
- Stand next to best man at the altar
- Escort bridesmaid down aisle during the recessional (follow maid of honor and best man)
- Remove pew ribbons and roll up aisle runner
- Accompany bride and groom for pictures

At the Reception

- Sit at either end of the head table next to assigned bridesmaid
- Dance with bridesmaid during the formal dance introducing wedding party

Bridesmaid (photocopy if more than one)

Arrival time: _____

Location: _____

Other: _____

At the Ceremony

- Assist with last-minute preparations
- Help keep track of belongings in dressing room
- Receive bouquet at bride's house and help florist pass out flowers
- Follow flower girl/ring bearer and precede maid of honor down the aisle at the start of the ceremony
- Accompanied by groomsman, follow maid of aisle down the aisle after ceremony
- Accompany bride and groom for pictures

At the Reception

- Stand in the receiving line next to the maid of honor
- Sit at either end of the head table next to assigned groomsman
- Dance with groomsman during the formal dance introducing wedding party

Bride's Parents

Arrival time: _____

Location: _____

Other: _____

Before the Ceremony
- Bride's mother leaves the house first with bridesmaids; father follows in separate car with bride

At the Ceremony
- Bride's mother is seated just prior to processional
- Bride's father escorts bride down the aisle, then joins mother in first pew to the left
- Parents exit church together after recessional
- Accompany bride and groom for pictures

At the Reception
- Bride's mother stands first in receiving line, next to either the groom's mother or the bride's father
- Bride's mother is seated next to groom's father and opposite bride's father at table
- Father of the bride's first dance is with groom's mother and the mother of the bride's is with the groom's father
- Parents may host post-wedding party at their house

Groom's Parents

Arrival time: _____

Location: _____

Other: _____

Before the Ceremony
- Groom's parents arrive at church prior to other bridal party members (except groom and ushers)

At the Ceremony
- Just prior to seating mother of bride, an usher escorts mother of groom down the aisle and seats her in first pew on right
- Father of the groom follows, alone
- Parents exit church together after recessional
- Accompany bride and groom for pictures

At the Reception
- Groom's mother stands next to either the bride's mother or the groom's father in receiving line
- Groom's mother is seated next to bride's father and opposite groom's father at table
- Father of the bride's first dance is with groom's mother and the mother of the bride's is with the groom's father

Ring Bearer

Arrival time: _____

Location: _____

Other: _____

At the Ceremony
- Carry bride's wedding band (or a symbolic ring) on a pillow down the aisle
- Precede flower girl(s) and bride and her father during processional
- May stand at altar or sit in bride's mother's pew just before reaching the altar
- Remain seated during recessional
- Accompany bride and groom for pictures

Flower Girl

Arrival time: _____

Location: _____

Other: _____

At the Ceremony
- Carry basket of petals and scatter them on the aisle runner
- Proceed bride and her father during processional
- May stand at altar or sit in bride's mother's pew just before reaching the altar
- Follow bride and groom during recessional
- Accompany bride and groom for pictures